THE VENICE EXPERIMENT

THE VENICE EXPERIMENT

A Year of Trial and Error Living Abroad

by Barry Frangipane
with Ben Robbins

The Venice Experiment

Copyright © 2011 by Barry Frangipane and Ben Robbins

Editor: Lynn O'Dell

ISBN 978-0-9836141-1-1 (HC)   978-0-9836141-0-4 (PB)

Library of Congress Control Number 2011907814

Library of Congress Cataloging-in-Publication Data

Frangipane, Barry.   Robbins, Ben.

The Venice Experiment: A Year of Trial and Error Living Abroad / by Barry Frangipane with Ben Robbins.

1. Venice (Italy)--Description and travel.

2. Venice (Italy)--Humor. 3. Venice (Italy) --Social life and customs.

www.SavoryAdventuresPublishing.com

First Printing, 2011

TABLE OF CONTENTS

ACKNOWLEDGEMENTS

I must extend my thanks for the help and inspiration that made this book possible: To Carolyn Rosser, the neighbor who saved the stories we emailed while living in Venice, bound them, and gave them to me upon our return with a cover titled, "I Could Write a Book," and so I did; to my daughters Amber and Stephanie who encouraged me by giving me blank journals with instructions to fill them with stories; to Ben Robbins who has heard me tell each of these stories, putting him in the position to enhance this book with the colorful parts I did not write down, and to the one and only Dolce Debbie, my wife, for supporting me through countless hours of writing and loving me even after I included her in this true story of our lives together in Venice.

FOREWORD

Sixteen hundred years ago, in the year 452, two Italian guys walked into a bar—bear with me here—mourning their town's imminent destruction at the hands of Attila the Hun and his ferocious army.

As they drowned their sorrows, one of them turned to the other and said, "Attilla has already ransacked the north from Paris to Strasbourg, and is heading towards Italy. If we don't do something, he'll get us too. But I've got an idea. Let's cut down millions of big trees, and then float them two miles out into the lagoon. We'll pound the trunks down into the muck around a sandbar, and then on top of this foundation, we'll build a huge new town out of granite and marble from the mainland. The Huns won't be able to get us out there."

"But," the other guy said, "chainsaws won't be invented for another fifteen hundred years, and all we have are these little wooden boats."

"Non ti preoccupare," the first guy said. "Don't worry. I've got an axe, and I just sharpened it this morning."

"Sounds good to me," answered his friend. They and all their buddies then proceeded to drink massive quantities of alcohol until they actually believed that this was a perfectly logical plan for defending against an onslaught of vicious invaders.

Fast forward to the twenty-first century. Every year, twenty million visitors marvel at the sheer genius of this magnificent city that still stands above the water—most of the time – on these same ancient tree trunks. To be sure, the first Venetians had no idea their island would someday be one of the epic wonders of the world, but history now regards this axe guy in the bar as a true visionary. He tried something different, something seemingly impossible, convinced a group of people to join him, and it all worked out brilliantly.

My friend Barry Frangipane is another such contrarian. After sixteen years of his mother insisting that dessert had to come after dinner, one day he tried it the other way around, and this new order has worked just fine ever since. Not quite brilliant perhaps, but a valuable lesson nonetheless.

I got to know Barry when he was nearly fifty and was immediately struck by his possession of two rare qualities— an absolute disregard for convention and an uncanny gift for connecting with people. For the last several years, I have been the beneficiary of both.

During our work together, he has shared story upon story over lunches and late nights at the office. For a guy only twenty years my senior, it seems like he has a century's worth of life experiences beyond my own.

FOREWORD

Barry's implausible successes inspire countless people to venture off the beaten path and discover a life beyond the comfort zone. In his failures, and there have been plenty, he manages to extract and share valuable lessons that are more often than not hysterical. His brand of fearlessness is a rare breath of fresh air in our modern risk-averse society.

In a world of nearly seven billion strangers, Barry deliberately takes the time to connect with nearly every human being who passes within ten feet or so. A few find this unsettling, but it makes a delightful and lasting impression on so many others. For Barry, each encounter fills in another detail in a lifelong tapestry of relationships.

It's not without a bit of jealousy that I enjoy Barry's tales of traveling the world, mastering new languages, making friends, and starting crazy ventures. He's always off to do remarkable things that people like you and I can't just run off and do—or can we?

This book is the record of Barry's love affair with Venice, including the year that he spent living and working there. It's just one of his endless series of experiments with cultural habits and human interaction. Personally, I find his observations both insightful and encouraging. I hope you enjoy meeting him as much as I have.

~Ben Robbins

1

LEAVING HOME

My secret plan to move to Venice was ready. It was time to see if my wife would buy into the idea of leaving our home to live for an entire year in a foreign country.

As happens from time to time in the sunshine state, dark thunderclouds had formed over our suburban tropical paradise with little warning. I had been reviewing software code on our patio as I waited for Debbie to return home. The steady rain turned to a thick spray as it came through the screened enclosure, and the water in the swimming pool gradually overflowed, rippling onto the deck.

Debbie entered the house with water dripping from her clothing, and fought to close her broken umbrella. Her five-inch Manolos, covered with mud, were kicked across the kitchen floor. I closed my eyes for a moment, wondering if this might be a bad day to tell her of my plan. The sound of ice clinking against a glass told me Debbie was certainly pouring her drink of choice, Grey Goose. Comfortable in my armchair, I smiled as my wife told me about her terrible day, and my imagination filled in the details...

———————————

When Debbie left her office for the evening, a gust of wind blew the papers composing her night's project from her hands into the swampy ditch alongside the road. Her thin skirt flapped violently around her waist as she bent over on the roadside. Drenched from the horizontal Florida rain and wind, she ignored the long line of slowly moving cars behind her. Her umbrella had escaped and blown across the nearby parking lot. Water began to gather in the ditch, so she lunged farther in, desperately grasping at escaped sheets of paper caught in the weeds.

The droplets of rain weren't particularly heavy, but with every gust, they stung her mascara-streaked face like tiny needles. Clutching a handful of soggy paperwork against her rain-drenched silk blouse, she gritted her teeth and ignored the first few horn blasts. Her Manolo Blahnik heels sank into the brown muck as she made her way back and forth across the ditch

As she snatched up the last remaining sheets, more honking and finally a catcall rang out from a pickup truck waiting at the light. The grinning man in the driver's seat recoiled as Debbie's head whipped around to reveal an angry glare framed with rain-matted auburn hair. A sudden blast of wind drowned out whatever she screamed at him while extending the middle finger of a hand that still clutched a soggy mass of papers.

"It sounds like you had a pretty bad day," I said, as Debbie continued her story.

"Every damned report in here is trashed," she declared, sinking back into the overstuffed chair with a sigh. "I can't do anything with these till tomorrow. They're pointless anyhow; nobody really needs them. I hate this hellhole of a job."

"If they're pointless, why stress out over them," I offered. "Look at it this way, now you don't have to work tonight."

Clearly not amused, Debbie stared sullenly into space. I took a deep breath and closed my laptop. It was time. Of all the days to finally tell her what I had been secretly plotting....

I began, "Debbie, I've been thinking about maybe the two of us going somewhere."

"Good Lord, what have you come up with this time?" She peered at me suspiciously over her glass. "Barry, the last time you said that, we disappeared to Paris for two weeks. How are we supposed to do that now? We have jobs, and I'm way too far behind right now…" Her voice trailed off as though she hadn't completely convinced herself.

"Well, you didn't seem too attached to your job a second ago," I countered. "None of my clients are here in Florida, and they don't know where I'm connecting from."

In an annoyed tone, she responded, "Why the hell would you want to go on vacation if you're just going to work?" Her confusion was understandable. It was time to tip my hand.

"I'm not talking about a vacation."

Setting down her glass, Debbie leaned forward intently. Confident I had her attention, I continued to tease her by stating the obvious. "So, since I'm not where they are, and they're not where we are, it doesn't matter where we live, does it?"

Debbie blinked, waiting for some indication of my intentions. "Damn it, Barry, what are you trying to say?"

"Well, I've been looking at apartments in this little town called," I paused, "Venice." Unable at this point to suppress my ear-to-ear grin, I continued, "We can get

4

a place on the island. I'll bring my laptop and internet phone, and I can work afternoons. My clients will never even know we moved, and we can rent the house out. Since it's Venice, we certainly won't need cars. We'll sell them both, and with the money we save on payments, insurance, gas, and repairs, we can live on just one salary—mine."

"We could do it for a year. You can just relax and cook— with better ingredients than you have here. You'd rather be doing that anyhow, right?" After months of planning, I was satisfied that I had thought of virtually everything.

Debbie took a deep breath and settled back in her chair. For a split second, I found myself unsure that my scheme was unfolding as planned. Doing her best to muster a poker face, she responded, "Huh. You're actually serious? You want to just pack up and move to a foreign country?"

"Well, yeah. Unless you'd rather just stay here."

Her face suddenly looked distant, and for a moment, I couldn't tell how she felt about my proposition. It was my turn to blink. "So... what do you think? Are you in or not?"

Staring coolly at me, Debbie hesitated, sensing my anticipation and relishing the moment. The slightest hint of a smile appeared, and no amount of determination could hide the growing excitement in her eyes.

"I'm in!" she suddenly squealed, clapping her hands together like a little girl. "I quit, I quit! I swear, we're gonna do this!" Gradually regaining her composure, she settled into a slow bouncing motion in the chair.

"So," she wondered out loud, "what kind of an apartment do you think we can get?" Debbie wandered off to search Google for apartment rentals in Venice.

I contentedly basked in the success of my plan. At an early age, I had realized that not everyone had a high tolerance for my spontaneous ideas. I felt especially lucky to have a wife who actually seemed to enjoy my spur-of-the-moment inspirations, and who helped me to better pace my impulses. For her part, Debbie was well aware of how unpredictable life with me could be, since our relationship itself had been based on spontaneity from the start.

Our paths had converged ten years earlier in the summer of 1996, when I was still adjusting to life as a single parent to my two daughters, Stephanie and Amber. Selling my stake in the software company I co-founded a decade earlier had given me more time to spend with my girls. I worked on my consulting practice mostly from home, using an internet phone to stay in touch with a small group of clients scattered across the United States.

I had been working in my den on a Thursday morning, sipping coffee, when the phone rang.

"Hey, darlin', it's Debbie!" Even though we had never met in person, her Texas drawl was familiar and friendly. "The system is acting up again."

Although I worked closely with all of my clients, there was a certain electricity in the air when I heard this particular voice. Debbie was responsible for payroll on a construction site at the Anheuser Busch brewery in Houston. There was always something special about her calls. It might have been the way she called me "Darlin'," even though she called everyone else that, too. Whatever it was, I looked forward to any chance to speak to her and found myself always willing to spend any amount of time helping her.

I listened patiently as Debbie described the problem with her computer. She concluded with, "I swear, you probably think I make this stuff up just so I can call and bug you."

Recalling that my girls were staying with their grandparents over the weekend, I sensed an opportunity, and immediately volunteered, "Debbie, I don't think I can fix this one from here, but I can come out Saturday and get it taken care of."

Surprised, she answered cautiously, "Um, okay."

"I'll need someone to pick me up."

"I guess that'll be me. How will I recognize you at the airport?"

"I'll be the all-white guy wearing all black," I responded, impressed with my own cleverness.

Forty-eight hours later, my heart pounded as my early flight touched down in Houston. I was surprisingly nervous about meeting this woman I had known only as a friendly voice on the phone for the last several months, and had no idea what to expect.

As I deplaned, the only person waiting was a stunning redhead in black jeans and a tight-fitting blouse. She examined each person through her dark sunglasses as they emerged from the jetway. As I nervously walked toward her with my bag in tow, she watched me curiously, finally asking, "Barry? Is that you?"

I was still in awe, and blurted out the only thing I could think of, "Uh, yeah. That's me, the all-white man in all black."

"Oh, my God," she squealed, giving me a quick hug. "I'm so glad to finally meet you!"

Stepping back, she put her hands on her hips and looked me up and down, her gaze finally settling on my nondescript black suitcase affixed with a large label that read *THIS IS NOT YOUR BAG*. Chuckling and shaking her head, she turned toward the exit. "Alright, let's get goin'."

I followed as she led the way at an impressive pace for someone in four-inch heels. Hurrying to keep up, my eyes were locked on her shape, while I attempted to conceal my admiration. As we threaded our way through the crowd toward the parking garage, she glanced over her shoulder a few times to ensure I was keeping up. Each time she looked, I would quickly try to suppress the enormous grin that had planted itself on my face.

Debbie unlocked her little Toyota Corolla, and we jumped in. Screeching around the parking garage's circular ramp, it was immediately clear why the car was missing two hubcaps. Still grinning with nervous excitement, I gripped the door handle as we sped away from the airport. It was the most fun I could remember having in years.

We made our way along the highway into the city. Eager to make conversation, I asked, "So, other than the system going down, how was your week?"

"Oh, you mean other than the whole system crashin', me dumpin' my boyfriend, and feelin' like hell after gettin' totally trashed with the girls last night?" She pulled her sunglasses down to glare at me with bloodshot eyes.

Wishing that I hadn't asked, I simply replied, "Well, I guess you're looking forward to a productive weekend then." I then stared directly ahead, contemplating what might be a safer topic.

We arrived at the brewery and walked through the plant to her office, which was located in a small trailer adjacent to the brewery. As she unlocked the door, her face practically turned green from the smell of fresh hops. After showing me where her computer was located, she quickly excused herself, clearly still feeling the effects of the night before. When she returned fifteen minutes later, I proudly showed off her fully repaired system.

"That didn't take long," she remarked suspiciously. "There's not much to see in Houston on a Saturday. How about a late lunch?" She suggested that I might enjoy a local Mexican restaurant, although she seemed less than excited by the thought of food. Despite her gastrointestinal handicap, several beers and margaritas later, we were the best of friends. For nearly four hours, we talked about food, friends, and life in general. I learned that she was a classically trained pianist who loved to cook, and that she had always wanted to travel. I told her about my first marriage falling apart, and she bashfully shared her childhood dream of marrying an Italian who would whisk her away to the Mediterranean coast.

Finally, realizing that it was early evening, she said, "It's gettin' late. What hotel are you staying at?"

Mustering my best straight face, I countered, "Well, this is Houston; there's bound to be some place to sleep, right?"

The following morning, as we left her apartment to drive back to the airport, we agreed to see each other again the following weekend. Two months later, Debbie moved to Florida, and we began planning our first trip to Europe together.

On our first date in Houston, Debbie had revealed her dreams of romance and Prince Charming. I, however, had my own ideas about what a perfect life companion required—someone with the stamina to survive both the good days and the bad. It was therefore no accident that I made her first trip to Europe a whirlwind of activity.

Whether or not she realized it, my new love interest underwent a rigorous test of endurance. Having spent much of my life traveling, it was important to me to find out whether she could keep up the grueling pace of constantly being on the move and adjusting for the unexpected. Our itinerary consisted of four countries in ten days. We would tour France, Austria, and Switzerland, sleeping along the way on trains and in hostels. We would end in Italy, where we would stay with my mother's relatives.

From the start, it was clear that Debbie was not only a great companion, but also a natural traveler. We picnicked at the Jardin du Luxembourg in Paris and walked along Champs Elysées exploring the boutiques, galleries, and cafés. She reveled in the glamour and fashions of Paris, but seemed just as content curled up in my arms on the train as we left. The more time we spent together, the more I marveled at the calming effect Debbie had on me. In Salzburg, Austria, we ran down hundreds of steps in a thunderstorm from the castle to the hostel, sampling the apple strudel at every café along the way.

In Switzerland, as we watched our missed train pull away from Lugano station, I banged my fists on the wall. Debbie just put her arm around my waist and whispered, "Darlin', what's the worst thing that's gonna happen? If we have to spend four more hours here feeding the swans and walking around the lake, I'm okay with that."

I was more relaxed than ever as we embarked on the last leg of our trip. While on the next train to Italy, I phoned ahead to my relatives to arrange for them to pick us up at the station. Conversations in Italian, especially by phone, were difficult for me. After listening to many Italian language tapes over the years, I had learned enough of the language to ask questions, but often didn't understand the answers. My uncle understood, I had hoped, that we would be arriving on the next train from Lugano. We exited the train in Conegliano, Italy, to find my aunt and uncle waiting on the platform. Zio Alfieri was a proud man, short, with a long, curly mustache that barely hid his smile. Over the years since I met him, his physique had certainly changed from that of a soccer player to a soccer coach. Even in middle age, though, the twinkle in his eyes, together with his strong handshakes and hugs, still revealed both a strong physical work ethic and a warm character.

In terrible Italian, I did my best to introduce Debbie. While I was explaining to Debbie that *zio* meant *uncle* and *zia* meant *aunt*, Zio Alfieri carefully examined her physical attributes before turning to nod approvingly and say, "Bravo! Bravo, Barry!"

He then excitedly relayed something in Italian to my aunt, who looked at me and smiled. Without understanding a word, we both knew that Debbie had passed the initial audition. Zia Loredana laughed. "Alfieri appreciates the beautiful women," she said as she gave Debbie a big hug. My uncle and I worked on loading the luggage into his tiny Fiat, while attempting to save some space for the passengers.

After piling into the car, we set off toward their home in the village of Sarmede. With the stunning Dolomite Mountains as a backdrop, we drove through the rolling hills until a group of homes and businesses clustered around a church came into view. My aunt explained to Debbie that this small town of three thousand people was where she and my mother were born and raised.

After arriving at their home, Debbie was introduced to my uncle's elderly mother, Zia Agosta. They then escorted us back outside to a small attached apartment with two rooms—a combination kitchen/dining room downstairs with a spiral staircase leading to a room containing a queen-size bed and small bath.

"Barry's mother was born right here in this apartment," Zia Loredana explained to Debbie in Italian, with me translating as much as I could understand. "For the next few days, the two of you will stay here."

Behind us, a concerned voice asked, "But where will Barry sleep?" We turned to see Zia Agosta behind us. In her generation, the very suggestion of an unmarried couple sleeping together was preposterous.

Zia Loredana winked at me and explained to her mother-in-law, "Barry will sleep on the kitchen table downstairs, and Debbie will sleep in the bed upstairs."

Zia Agosta seemed satisfied with that answer. A few hours later, she knocked on the door of the apartment carrying extra blankets and a pillow to ensure that I would be comfortable on the table.

The next morning, we joined the family for a breakfast of local cheeses and breads, and Zia Agosta inquired as to how I was feeling. While starting to tell her how refreshed I was, I felt an elbow in my ribs and heard Zia Loredana's "Ahem."

Alerted to my near undoing, I quickly groaned, held my side, and demonstrated the proper amount of aches and pains for someone who had spent the night on the kitchen table. Zio Alfieri chuckled under his breath, then made an announcement about the morning's plans that had something to do with the local market and walked outside.

"What did he say?" Debbie asked.

"I'm not sure. He either said we are all going to the market, or we all went to the market. I still have trouble distinguishing between the past and future tenses." Loredana and Zia Agosta joined Alfieri outside.

"Since we haven't been to the market, he must have said that we're going now. Look out the window; I think they're waiting for us," Debbie said.

We walked toward the car. Scrutinizing Debbie's short, white sundress, a concerned Zia Agosta asked, "Isn't Debbie going to change before we go to the market?"

Zio Alfieri let out an audible groan. Debbie, stunned, hurried back into the apartment to change into something more conservative that would satisfy the censors.

It was clearly market day in Vittorio Veneto, as tiny cars lined every inch of available roadside. Alfieri found a perfect parking spot on the sidewalk. In this hillside town, the community parking area had been taken over with vendors with local cheeses from Piancavallo, barrels of green olives, antiques, and new CDs with music from all the latest Italian singers.

After walking downhill through a mile of street vendors, we walked back uphill, returning to the car with no one having purchased anything.

After we finished shopping, we dropped off Zia Agosta at the house. The rest of us drove to the hill town of San Daniele and found a table where we could relax in the sun and enjoy some prosciutto and Prosecco, a sparkling white wine similar to champagne. San Daniele, a quiet little spot in the foothills of the picturesque Dolomites, was home to arguably the best prosciutto in Italy. Tiny restaurants specializing in the local delicacy were found on every corner. Many of them offered beautiful views from outside terraces, where thin slices of prosciutto were served on silver platters paired with homemade *grissini* breadsticks and white wine.

We sat and talked, taking in the view as we recalled the morning's events. As young women strolled by, one after the other with short skirts and bare shoulders, Zio Alfieri nodded approvingly, while Debbie just watched, perplexed, thinking about her required change of clothing earlier in the day.

It was very tiring listening to every word in a foreign conversation, just hoping to glean a clue as to the topic. So the more the meal dragged on, the more I ignored the conversation entirely. At one point, however, Alfieri must have told a joke, as he and Loredana both started laughing, then looked over at me expectantly. Naturally, I laughed too, not wanting them to think that I wasn't listening. Debbie asked, "What did they say?" The table was silent.

While my aunt and uncle certainly didn't know enough English to understand Debbie's question, based on her timing and perplexed look, they knew what she was asking. I had to think fast.

"Debbie, here's what happened. Alfieri said something, then Loredana responded, then Alfieri said something else, and they both laughed. At this point you need to burst into laughter, or they'll know I have no clue what they said." Debbie burst into laughter, as did Alfieri, Loredana, and I, although for different reasons.

The next morning, we said our goodbyes to the family and set out to spend the last days of our trip in Venice. Debbie pressed her nose against the window as the train skimmed across the lagoon toward the island. Slowly, Venice came into view. All the bell towers seemed to grow as we neared the city, with the famous *campanile* towering over Saint Mark's Square.

As we left the station, the city of water opened itself up to us. The Grand Canal, directly ahead, was bustling with activity. Two *vaporetto*, or waterbus, stops perched on the edge of the canal with people waiting at each one. We watched people going about mundane daily routines in this exotic place that seemed to emerge directly out of the sea. Traveling down the canal were merchant boats carrying wine, toilet paper, and Coke, while a UPS boat delivered packages to businesses on the canal. Palaces rose up from the water with beautiful blown-glass chandeliers glistening in the windows. The aroma of fresh pastries filled the air.

Debbie stopped at the edge of the Grand Canal and began to cry. "I never dreamed," she sobbed. "Seeing it in pictures and in movies, you just have no clue. I feel like I'm finally at home."

We got to the end of the line to board Vaporetto #1, the waterbus that ran the entire length of the Grand Canal. As we waited, little old men with newspapers and old ladies with grocery bags bypassed our line, creating a mass of people in disarray at the dock. When the *vaporetto* arrived, the crowd boarded the boat leaving us, and others, behind. As the boat left the dock and motored down the canal, we decided to tour Venice on foot instead.

Determined to make the most of our one day, we wandered the streets and squares, visiting all six *sestieri,* sections, of the city. In this town of almost four hundred pedestrian bridges and no cars, we crossed bridge after bridge, really going nowhere in particular. On the banks of a small canal, furniture was being loaded onto one boat, while on the other side of the canal, fresh fish was being unloaded from another. Small stores lined the *calli,* or walkways. One butcher shop sold only poultry, the next sold only beef and pork. Small delicatessens with beautiful Italian cold cuts like *Prosciutto, Mortadella,* and *Sopressata* called to us. It was amazing how many products they could stock in a store the size of an average American living room.

Gondolas crisscrossed the Grand Canal dodging larger boats delivering wine, produce, and dry cleaning. The centuries-old palaces lining the canal seemed to be leaning on each other for support, some more successfully than others.

One of the biggest surprises was a huge park called the Giardini Pubblici with its expansive walks under hundreds of tall trees and benches lining the way. We would have never dreamt that in a city built mostly on tree trunks pounded into the ground, there would be a park almost half the size of the famous Luxembourg Gardens in Paris.

On a tip from my friend Giorgio, we searched for a particular *gelateria* in the Santa Croce neighborhood that he promised served Venice's best *gelato*, a frozen dessert similar to ice cream but made with milk rather than cream. The address led us to a small, unassuming storefront near Ponte degli Scalzi, one of only three bridges crossing the Grand Canal, with no outside sign to indicate that it was in fact Gelateria Alaska, the name we were given, or that it was a *gelateria* at all.

Pressing our noses to the glass, we peered through the dust to see a large map of Jamaica on one wall and a photo of Bob Marley on the other. The ice cream display was empty, the door was locked, and there was a large handwritten sign on the door that read, "*Chiuso a causa di malattia*," which I translated as "Closed due to illness."

We were becoming accustomed to these dead ends—a surprising number of stores were closed in the middle of the day—but this one was different. There were over forty comments handwritten by customers and friends on the weather-beaten sign.

Guarisci presto, Carlo—Get well soon, Carlo—and *Torna subito mio grande amico*—Return soon, my good friend—read the first few comments that I translated roughly for Debbie.

The thought of poor Carlo suffering made us suddenly realize that this magical place was full of people making their way through life like they do any other place on earth. The outpouring of concern scrawled on the window made us imagine the kind of friendship that Carlo must have had with his clients, and how closely knit the neighborhood must be.

As if she could read my mind, Debbie asked, "Why don't you write something?"

I wrote it in English, hoping he would understand this note from a complete stranger. "Get well soon, Carlo. I can't wait to try your gelato!"

By this time, the sun was hanging low in the sky, and all of the other shops around us had also closed. Soaking in every detail along the way, Debbie and I slowly made our way back toward our hotel. I thought to myself how glad I was that this was the last stop on our trip. Had we begun in Venice, I wasn't sure we ever would have left.

The next afternoon, as our return flight took off, we banked hard over Venice. I leaned over to join Debbie in peering down as the city on the water disappeared into the distance. Somehow, even though we were headed home, it felt as though we were leaving something precious behind.

Not too differently from our own romance, Debbie and I had fallen in love at first sight with Venice and never quite recovered. We would make several return trips over the next decade, some lasting as long as a month. As much as we loved our home, friends, and family in Florida, leaving Venice was always difficult. This time, though, we would stay an entire year, enjoying the city at a relaxed pace without a looming departure date. It would be perfect.

2

BECOMING ILLEGAL IMMIGRANTS

Now that we were moving to Italy and becoming immigrants, I thought back to the 1930s when my mother came to America as an Italian immigrant. How ironic it was that I was filling out the paperwork to return to her homeland.

No one paid much attention to the comings and goings of tourists who only visited for a few weeks or less. However, as Italian residents for a year, we would need proper visas.

Knowing that the Italian consulate's office in Miami was usually the first stop for Floridians who wanted to stay for an extended time in Italy, I had prepared by checking their website for the list of items we would need.

Arriving at the consulate, we were relieved to see that that there was no line, and a guard ushered us in immediately. A well-dressed man behind a desk stood and greeted us. We sat nervously for a few minutes as he looked over our paperwork, nodded, and then reviewed it again.

Finally, he looked up and smiled. "Very good."

Debbie and I glanced at each other, relieved. Suddenly, he cocked his head to one side and asked, "Where is your lease for an apartment?"

My heart sank. I explained that we didn't yet have an apartment. We would begin looking for a place to live as soon as we had visas, I told him. After all, why would we sign a lease for an apartment without even having visas to stay in the country?

"No," he said. "Your visa will be issued for the same length of time as your lease. No lease, no visa." I assured him that if we simply stayed with friends, they would not require a lease.

"Then they will have to issue you a lease and have it registered with the city, just like everybody else. Come back when you have a lease."

Finding an Apartment

Debbie and I came to grips with the fact that we would have to postpone the move, but we were determined to clear the final hurdles as quickly as possible. The lease was our first priority, since it was needed before we could get visas. This meant, of course, that one of us had to go to Venice in person. We decided I would go to Venice alone to find an apartment and secure the lease. Upon my return, we would prepare to go back together with all of our things and the pets.

Two weeks later, I arrived in Venice. Crossing the bridge from the mainland, I simultaneously felt a rush of excitement and a twinge of guilt at enjoying Venice while Debbie was still in Florida. Reminded of my mission, determined not to be distracted by the sights and sounds surrounding me, I immediately set out to see my realtors.

Teresa and Elisabetta, or Betta, as I knew her, had helped us find wonderful apartments for our month-long stays in the past. Together with Raffaella, Betta's twin sister, they worked in an office on Strada Nova in the Cannaregio section of Venice. During each of our three previous stays, their agency had found us a wonderful apartment in which to vacation. This time, however, we needed something different, something better suited to a long stay. This time, we needed a *home*.

Betta—I'm almost sure it wasn't Raffaella—and I made our way over several bridges to see three apartments in Santa Croce, one of the less touristy neighborhoods of Venice. The first apartment was only a one bedroom, and having no separate place to work ruled that one out. The next apartment was on the fourth floor of a building with no elevator. While it was a bit larger, the thought of going up and down four flights of stairs every time we had to take our dog for a walk made it less than ideal.

Finally, Betta showed me a two-bedroom, ground-floor apartment in Santa Croce. It was small, but amply furnished, and overlooked a private courtyard with a weeping willow leaning over a canal. The landlord assured me that Santa Croce was a quiet part of town. The neighborhood contained only apartments; no noisy bars or restaurants would disturb us. Betta and I thought that it was the perfect place not only for Debbie and me, but also for our dog, Freckles, and cat, Alexandria. As a corner apartment, one side was directly on the small canal, ten inches above the waterline, and the other opened onto a dead-end calle, typical of Venice's many narrow walkways. Living on the ground floor would mean no stairs to traverse when taking Freckles for her many walks. Indeed, the apartment seemed almost perfect... except for one thing.

"Where is the oven?" I asked.

"Why do you need an oven?" Betta curiously asked.

"I just keep pots and pans in my oven," the landlord chimed in helpfully. Now it was my turn to be confused.

I explained that we weren't vacationing, but would be staying for an entire year and would need to cook. To the landlord's amusement, my realtor explained that very few Venetians used ovens in their homes.

"If you have a large meal to cook, you just ask a friend with a restaurant to use their oven," the landlord added matter-of-factly.

"Or better yet," Betta said, "just go out to eat!"

In the end, the landlord agreed to get us a small combination microwave and convection oven, which was a relief. Debbie wouldn't have been happy to discover she would be spending the next year without an oven.

In filling out the lease, the landlord asked Betta my name. "Frangipane, Barry," Betta replied. "Barry? What's that? Is that a name?"

"It's an American name," Betta explained, almost apologetically. "They don't always use names from the Bible." The landlord looked confused. Since my middle name is Joseph, I suggested that she add *Giuseppe*. "Frangipane, Barry Giuseppe." The landlord smiled and filled out the forms as *Barry Giuseppe Frangipane*, a real name, even if it wasn't exactly my real name.

I signed the papers that would finally allow us to move at the end of September. Remembering the no-nonsense clerk at the Italian Consulate's office in Miami, I verified its legitimacy. "This is a completely legal lease, right?"

"Oh, yes, this is a typical lease, widely used here in Venice," Betta assured me. I was ecstatic; the first hurdle had been crossed! The landlord bid us farewell with a wave and a smile.

As we walked away from the apartment, I felt a sharp pain as something fell from above, striking me on the shoulder before shattering on the street. Shocked, I rubbed my shoulder as I searched above for the culprit.

"It's just plaster from the building." Betta shrugged as though it was nothing out of the ordinary. As we made our way back, she explained that because Venice is surrounded by water, the buildings are in a constant state of decay. Property owners perform expensive periodic maintenance in an attempt to keep the deterioration in check, but the slowly crumbling architecture was just a fact of life to Venetians. She smiled at my apprehensive expression. "It's been this way for centuries. You'll get used to it."

A few turns later, I thanked Betta for her help, and we parted ways. *"Arrivederci, Giuseppe,"* she called as I walked away. I waved, wondering whether she found my new name as amusing as I did.

My next errand was to rent a Venetian post office box for a year. This, I thought, would be a far simpler way to get mail than to have it delivered to the apartment. I had read that until you were registered with the city as living in a particular apartment, the postman would not deliver your mail. Showing the necessary documents to the correct authorities, waiting for the registration to be processed, and following up on the process could take months; renting a post office box was preferable by far. Besides, with a Mailboxes, Etc. address, I would be sure my mail would be safely delivered even if I was traveling.

I arrived at the Mail Boxes Etc. store twenty minutes past noon only to find that they were closed for lunch from noon until three thirty in the afternoon. It was common in Venice for people to take lunch, and then settle in for an afternoon nap.

I returned to the store around three thirty and hung around until they reopened just before four o'clock. Entering the lobby, I carefully made my way around the piles of signs, boxes, and half-unpacked supplies, some new enterprise recently underway, I presumed.

A young man in his late twenties introduced himself as Cesare and proudly showed me his Mail Boxes Etc. store. I began to feel a bit of the recurring anxiety that seemed to accompany all of my preparations in Venice as he gave me the contract showing that my mailbox would be number 101. He confirmed my theory; mine would be the first mailbox in the store. Cesare had not yet completely unpacked his franchise kit, which was currently obstructing traffic through the lobby.

I signed the contract, paid him, and asked for the keys. My experience renting a mailbox at Mail Boxes Etc. in Florida led me to expect a key to my mailbox as well as a key to the front door that would allow me to enter the post office and check my mail at any time, day or night.

"All of the keys will be ready next week," he assured me. I agreed, but not without a growing feeling of apprehension. I was leaving for Florida the following morning, so the keys would have to wait until my return in September. I asked Cesare if there was anything else I needed to know.

"There are two postal codes for Cannaregio," he explained. "30121 and 30120. Be sure you use postal code 30121 for your mail."

The reason? "The postman for 30120 does not like our postman here in 30121. When the zip code is wrong, he sometimes keeps the mail for a few weeks before handing it over." Of course. Postal politics aside, it seemed that Cesare had everything under control. I felt somewhat reassured as I left.

That night, at an internet café, I ordered our new business cards online. "Barry and Debbie Frangipane, Box 101, Mail Boxes Etc, Cannaregio, 30121, Venice, Italy." We would hand them out to all of our friends and family members to be certain we would receive their mail while in Venice. I returned to Tampa triumphant, with lease in hand and a September move date in mind.

Debbie and I rushed to prepare. We held three garage sales and donated countless items to Goodwill. We would make the move with only the items we could bring on the plane or check as baggage. I would leave for Venice a week before Debbie, to ensure that everything was set before she arrived with the animals. Our daughter Stephanie agreed to travel with Debbie to help out with the move.

We received an email from our friends, Irene and Davide, in Venice. They would be getting married less than a week after I returned in September. Debbie would unfortunately miss the wedding, but the timing was perfect for me to attend.

Copies of the lease were sent via FedEx to the Italian Consulate's office in Miami. Time was getting tight, and it was important that the visas arrive in time for our departure. The following week, the packet we had been waiting for finally arrived. We rushed to open it and found a note written on our lease in large red marker: "Lease must be registered with the City of Venice. Application Denied."

Stunned, we called Betta in Venice, demanding to know why the landlord hadn't registered the lease. "No one wants to register a lease with the city because no one wants the income to be recorded," Betta explained. "If it was

registered, then they would be forced to pay income tax."
Debbie and I exchanged horrified glances. "In addition,
once the lease is registered with the city, it becomes almost
impossible to remove a tenant, even if they don't pay the
rent," the realtor explained. "We have checked with our
property owners, and they are not willing to register a
lease with the city."

"None of them?" I asked incredulously, glancing at my
wife. Debbie plopped down at my side, her face slack with
helplessness.

"I am sorry," Betta told me apologetically but firmly,
"none of them will do it." Numb with shock, I hung up the
phone. How could we move to Venice without visas?

Concerned friends and family encouraged us to
reconsider the move. After all, if navigating the law in
order to move was this difficult already, who knew what
legal complexities awaited us once we lived there?

We called Francesco, another friend in Venice, to ask
for advice. "Come over anyway," he responded simply,
without any concern for the legality of such a move. "No
one actually gets a visa. It is a good law, the one requiring a
visa," he assured us cheerfully, "but it is not very practical."

Francesco bade us farewell. *"Non ti preoccupare!* I
will see you in September."

Debbie and I looked down at the denied application for visas, looked at each other, and shrugged. What else could we do, but continue our preparations?

Over the following weeks, we performed a final inventory of our personal items to ensure nothing vital had been forgotten. Would the apartment already have towels and washcloths? Certain electronics, including my computer printer, modem, and cordless telephone, we would need, even though they were designed to work only with the 110 voltage current used in the United States. Could we live without Debbie's Kitchen Aid mixer?

After much hand wringing, we finally concluded that we would simply find replacement items in Venice for any household items. We laughed at our own anxiety, remembering that, after all, we weren't moving to a third world country.

Getting Freckles and Alexandria ready for the trip still required a series of properly choreographed and carefully documented steps to satisfy the authorities. One step out of order and the animals would not be allowed in Italy. Certain vaccines had to be applied months in advance, others over a period of time, and then others no more than ten days before departure. There were forms to be provided by our veterinarian, as well as the certificate from the USDA, available only after driving two hours to an office in Orlando.

Ever organized, Debbie managed to keep the process moving, although we were almost derailed when the vet got sick and moved our appointment to within one day of the strict deadline for the shots. Two months, two thousand dollars, and countless needles later, both animals were ready to go. With so many formalities, rules, and requirements, it was amazing that anyone could live in Italy.

"It's an active September in the tropics this year, and tropical storm Ivan is heading right for Jamaica," the TV weatherman said as I kissed Debbie goodbye to leave for the airport. *I'll be glad to get away from Florida's crazy weather*, I thought to myself as I dragged my six suitcases to the baggage handler at Tampa International Airport.

Hours later, somewhere over the Atlantic, my thoughts turned to what it would be like to finally live in Italy rather than just be a visitor. Sometimes figuring out the rules just required some perspective. I recalled my first trip to Italy and the seemingly impossible challenge of finding my family.

It had been a rainy evening almost thirty years earlier when the train wheels screeched on the metal rails as they slowly came to a stop in Treviso. My parents had arrived in Mamma's childhood town, located just twenty minutes north of Venice, the previous week. It was May of 1976 and my first time outside of the United States. The trip had been long, flying first from Tampa to Paris, then taking the train to Venice, and finally arriving in Treviso.

I was traveling alone and spoke no Italian, but the instructions my mother had written were simple enough. I was to get off the train, exit the station, and get on the Number 10 bus, giving the bus driver two fifty lire coins for a bus ticket. "Make sure you have two fifty lire coins, because the ticket machine on the bus only accepts exact change," Mamma had instructed. I was to get off the bus at Via Bibano, where I would recognize my aunt's house by the photograph in my pocket.

Leaving the train station, I remembered that I would need two fifty lire coins. Realizing I had no change, I looked down the street for a store of some kind, but the shops all appeared to be closed for the night. I recalled seeing a newsstand just off the train platform, so I hurried back inside the station.

The young lady was packing up for the night as I hurriedly gave her a five hundred lire note to purchase a newspaper. She gave me a couple of two hundred lire notes in return. Still, I had no change. I held up a pack of gum and handed her one of the 200 lire notes. She took the money and counted back five pieces of candy as change. Confused, I picked up a magazine for a hundred and fifty lire and put it on the counter with the remaining two hundred lire note. She promptly handed me ten more pieces of candy.

Stunned, I stared as she locked the register drawer and stepped out from behind the counter. "Ciao," she said with a smile, and then waved goodbye. My heart sank as I watched her walk away. Clearly, the candy was not going to get me on the bus.

Ready to cry, I walked outside and sat in the rain on the steps in front of the train station. Four thousand miles from home, tired, hungry, and roughly two miles in some direction from my aunt's house, I couldn't get on the bus. A tiny white car with the word "Taxi" on the side pulled alongside the curb at the bottom of the steps. The man in the driver's seat leaned over and stared up at me through the passenger window.

Unsure how to ask for help, but realizing this could be my only chance, I pulled the photo of my Aunt's house from my pocket.

"Via Bibano!" I said tentatively, displaying the photo of my intended destination. He nodded and leaned over to open the passenger door. Without another word, we were off. He seemed to know exactly where he was going. Exhausted, I just watched the houses and landscape go by.

Thirty minutes and nine thousand lire later, I was reunited with my parents and introduced to my aunts and uncles. Mamma helped to dry me off as I relayed the day's events.

She relayed my story about receiving candy instead of coins to Zio Meno, my uncle, a gregarious man who was always smiling. He laughed heartily, then led me into his room and opened the top drawer of a large dresser. It was *full* of coins! He explained something in Italian to my mother before bursting into laughter once again.

"There is a coin shortage in Italy," she translated. "Everyone is holding onto them so they don't run out!"

Zio Meno clapped his hand on my shoulder and advised me not to worry about finding change for the bus. "This is Italy. No one pays anyway," he assured me with a chuckle.

After dinner that night, my mother translated as Zio Meno introduced me to grappa, the local moonshine, and we toasted my first lesson in Italian economics and culture. I wondered then, too, how anyone could live in such a confusing place.

Thirty years after that first trip, comfortable in my seat on the plane, I smiled at my teenage naiveté. The coin shortage was long over, and it was now apartment leases that Italians hoarded. Perhaps nothing had really changed. Like Americans and everyone else, Italians had their reasons for doing things in a certain way. Would I learn to see things from their perspective? Given a whole year to figure things out, how hard could it possibly be?

3

SETTLING IN

My flight arrived at Venice's Marco Polo Airport at the same time as two other international flights; there were over seven hundred passengers and only two officers checking passports. I groaned; it would surely take the whole day for us to clear passport control. Just then, two more Italian passport control officers arrived to reduce the length of the line. Their method was a bit unorthodox. Pulling aside the rope barriers, they waved three hundred of us through without checking a single passport. In less than two minutes, they had cut the size of the line in half. I marveled at Italian efficiency at work; giving hardly a thought to the security risks, I hurried through the line alongside other travelers from several continents.

When I arrived by water taxi at our new apartment with all of my bags in tow, I was greeted by our landlord, Simonetta, and her middle-aged daughter. "My husband got the internet connection all set up in just two months," the daughter informed me happily, obviously quite proud of her spouse's accomplishment. "It was possible because he works for Telecom Italia."

I smiled appreciatively and thanked them, at the same time chuckling to myself at the fuss they made over something as simple as getting an internet connection. With unpacking, food shopping, appliance purchasing, and countless other tasks ahead of me, I was glad having utilities turned on was one thing I could take for granted.

I had barely opened the first bag when the landlord exclaimed, "Enough about the apartment, today is the *Regatta Storica!*" Though the Regatta Storica was one of Venice's great traditions and had been held annually for nearly five hundred years, I had never actually seen it in person. For this historic celebration of the annual rowing races, every year, brightly decorated sixteenth-century style boats glided up the Grand Canal in a colorful parade, guided by gondoliers in period dress.

"I have a seat saved for you on the Grand Canal," my landlord explained, "but we need to get there early." We walked a few blocks to the Grand Canal, where the residents had staked their claims on the best viewing spots by carefully positioning their folding chairs and blankets along the canal's edge.

Teams of *vogatori* rowed by in smaller sporting boats with all of the oarsmen wearing matching outfits representing their team, city, or country. If we clapped loud enough, a team would raise their oars into the air to salute us as they glided by. A light breeze on the sunny September day made the perfect backdrop for the historic regatta.

After watching the boats with Simonetta for an hour or so, I thanked her and went back to the apartment to set about unpacking and making a shopping list. In spite of our advance preparations, it seemed there were countless household items we needed to obtain before we could truly settle into our new home.

First, I purchased a *carello*, a small two-wheeled cart, which every Venetian owns. The *carello* is large enough to hold a typical day's groceries, but small enough to pull up and down the many pedestrian bridges between the store and home. After a few trips to secure some of the basics everyone needs, such as sugar, flour, salt, pepper, wooden spoons, dish soap, and shampoo, it was time to begin unpacking and finding a place for everything in the apartment.

The cheering of the crowds at the Grand Canal could be heard through my open window. I imagined Venice in the 1700s, with everyone dressed in those colorful outfits, cheering on their teams in the regatta. The ringing of my cell phone brought me back to the present. "Honey," Debbie greeted frantically, "that tropical storm has turned into a damn hurricane now, and it's heading straight at Florida."

"*Non ti preoccupare,*" I said confidently. "Those hurricanes never hit the Gulf Coast. Tampa will be fine." Debbie sounded less than reassured as I cheerfully said goodbye, adding, "See you in ten days!"

That first night, I lay in my bed, content to be in Venice, *La Serenissima*—the most serene, as it was called in the 1500s. Yes, it was a good life. Then, I was jarred from my musings by a recording of Dean Martin singing *Volare* that sounded like it was right outside my bedroom window. Looking out toward the canal, I saw a gondola full of tourists passing by with the CD player perched next to the gondolier. "Leave the confusion and all disillusion behind," Dean Martin sang winsomely. "Just like birds of a feather, a rainbow together we'll find..." Shaking my head, I went back to bed and drifted off to the crooning of "*Penso che un sogno cosi non ritornerá mai...*"

I woke early as the morning sun peeked over the wall of the courtyard. In spite of my many pressing errands, today wouldn't be a working day. This was the day our friends were getting married. I lay there thinking about our visit five years before, when we met a Venetian waitress named Irene. She worked in the *Ae Oche* pizzeria, appropriately situated on the *Calle delle Oche*, Street of the Geese, populated in centuries past by goose sellers.

Back then, Irene had just moved into an apartment with her boyfriend Davide. They were very much in love and excited about their new home, but very poor, with few furnishings for their apartment.

Each time we visited Venice, we would inevitably purchase items we needed during our weeks-long stay in an apartment. This usually included an assortment of linens, frying pans, china, and kitchen utensils. Rather than storing them or bringing them back with us to the U.S., we would give the items to Irene and Davide.

Today, they were getting married. My thoughts were interrupted by my phone vibrating on the chair I was using for a night table. The caller ID showed Debbie's cell phone number. Puzzled as to why she would be calling from her cell phone at more than two dollars a minute, I answered, "Yes, dear?"

"I'm sitting in the dark in the middle of a damn hurricane," Debbie said. "Hurricane Ivan is right on top of us, the power is out, the pool deck is flooded, and the water is leaking in through the glass doors!"

"Don't worry, hon. A week from now, you'll be here with me. Our apartment in Venice will be nice and dry. The electricity works, the weather is beautiful, and there are no leaks to worry about. Let the property manager take care of all that stuff after you leave," I offered comfortingly, feeling rather removed from her situation. There wasn't much else I could do from Venice. Besides, I had to get dressed for the wedding. After dressing for the morning's ceremony, I exited the apartment and greeted my landlord as she stood talking to a neighbor.

"How was your first night?" she queried.

I relayed my difficulty sleeping through the incessant music from the gondolas. "You'll get used to it," the landlord offered. "All the tourists want to hear *Volare*." I had to laugh. Tourists! I smiled smugly at the thought that I was no longer a visitor, but a true resident of Venice.

I headed down to the town hall near the Rialto Bridge, just as instructed on the invitation. There, we all stood together along the Grand Canal and waited in anticipation for the arrival of the bride, most of us, that is. Notably absent was Davide.

In Italy, timeliness is of little concern, even for life's most important events. Nonetheless, the crowd seemed to be getting nervous, and we were collectively relieved to see Davide finally hurrying down the *calle*. He tucked in his shirt as he drew near, smoothing down his hair, and muttering something about the *vaporetto* being late.

A few minutes later, family and friends cheered as Irene appeared in a rowboat decorated with white linens. I craned my neck to see as she was escorted onto the dock and upstairs into the town hall. As the bride turned to face us, I was surprised to see that she was glowing with pregnancy. Normally extremely slender, Irene appeared at first glance like a popsicle with her round, swollen belly atop skinny legs.

The ceremony was led by a young man in his early thirties, who had curly hair halfway down his back and was dressed in a white suit. A red, white, and green banner crossed his chest from the left shoulder to the right side of his waist with the word *"Magistrato"* stitched into it in large letters. After a speech in Venetian dialect, of which I understood not a word, the young man addressed Irene and Davide in an even longer speech, also in Venetian dialect. At the conclusion of the ceremony, the couple embraced in a long and passionate kiss. That part, I understood.

Back along the Grand Canal, bottles of sparkling Prosecco were opened and served in little plastic cups. The father of the groom offered a toast, and the couple disappeared into the crowd at the Rialto Bridge. The guests were instructed, thankfully in Italian, not in Venetian dialect, to meet them at the train station.

Thinking back to the part of the invitation I hadn't understood, I wondered about the location of the reception.

Another guest explained that we were to go to Irene's father's farm on the mainland. We would all take the train to Rovigo, and then would carpool the fifteen kilometers to the farm. A trip to the countryside hadn't been part of my plan, but I was committed to congratulating my friends on their wedding day.

After the forty-five minute train to Rovigo, I hitched a ride with four other partygoers. The car was a three-door Fiat Punto, one of Europe's famous 'supermini' cars, which comfortably seated only two people. Cramped but excited, the five of us made our way along various country roads for about fifteen minutes, no doubt consuming a thimble's worth of petrol.

The car stopped in a field in front of a small *agriturismo*, a sort of bed and breakfast run by families who turn their land into part farm, part hotel for tourists to help offset the bills.

The barn had been cleared, and tables set with white tablecloths, wine glasses, and china. The bride and groom, both vegetarians, obviously wanted to show their guests how good vegetarian food could be. Over the next few hours, we feasted on risotto with vegetables fresh from the farm, gnocchi with butter sauce and fried sage leaves, and beans in a tasty sauce, then finished with a delicate mascarpone cream. Davide, impressed with the chef's work, introduced him to the guests, and asked him what he used to make the beans so tasty. "Pork rinds. They made your vegetarian dish taste good, no?"

A stage had been erected outside the barn, and the Prosecco began to flow. Throughout the evening, we all danced under the stars to the music of the heavy rock band on stage. The elders were dressed in their Sunday finest, while Davide, Irene, and their friends had changed into t-shirts and jeans. I found the hearty Italian rendition of several heavily-accented Rolling Stones songs quite amusing.

It had been dark for some time when guests began to leave the barn. Worried that I might not find a ride back, I followed them outside. Davide approached and, putting his arm around my shoulder, said, "You must be very tired. Here, sleep." He handed me a dark bundle of cloth and plastic.

I must have made a funny face, because Davide laughed. "We're sleeping here." He pointed out at the field, where I now noticed guests setting up tents. "See you tomorrow," he said with a grin, then left to join his bride in the main house.

A few guests remained in the barn, but I stumbled out into the field and, finding a relatively flat spot, attempted to set up my tent in the dark. After semi-assembling it, I crawled inside and zipped the end shut. As soon as I rolled over, it collapsed on top of me. There was no sleeping bag, but it was a mild night, and the tent had me thoroughly cocooned. I lay there waiting for the music to stop, but the band played for at least another two hours. Finally, at roughly two in the morning, all was silent. Morning surely would come soon. It had to.

After daybreak, I lay there in my tent for an hour or so listening for any sign of others stirring. There was no movement. Finally, I crawled out, rolled my tent into a heap, and headed toward the barn looking for breakfast.

There were a few rolls left over from the night before. Downing them with flat Prosecco, I moved back and forth between the barn and tent to escape the mosquitoes, which seemed to be even hungrier than me. For two more hours, I sat in the barn watching the ten or fifteen tents out in the field. No one moved. There wasn't even a sound. I wondered whether everyone was simply sleeping in after drinking and smoking until three in the morning, or if somehow they had all gone home during the ten minutes I actually slept.

Suddenly, a girl in her early twenties appeared in the barn. Desperate for a way back to Venice, I approached her. She looked me over with some amusement as I explained my predicament. Her father was to come within an hour to take her to the train station. When he arrived, I desperately pleaded for a ride back to Rovigo. As we drove away, I looked back at the motionless tents in the field.

Whatever had happened to everyone else was a mystery I never solved. By three o'clock, I was back in Venice, tired and befuddled by the previous night's events, and wondering what I should do with the tent I had brought back with me.

No sooner had I returned from the farmlands of Rovigo to the civilization of Venice, than Debbie called to tell me about the latest hurricane. Our garden statues had toppled, barely missing the pool, and water was dripping onto the kitchen floor out of the speakers installed in the ceiling. Yawning, I did my best to reassure her, keeping my concerns about the state of Italy's collective insanity to myself. All I knew for certain was that I *had* to learn the language. As interesting and educational as the last twenty-four hours had been, I had no intention of going through a similar experience just because I didn't know how to read an invitation.

Still stiff from my night camping in a field, I was trying to get comfortable in the bed when the phone rang again.

"Ciao, Barry. It is Francesco. *Benvenuto in Italia!*" He explained that he was closing his bar for the evening, but his car was at Piazzale Roma. He needed to move it to a garage on the mainland because it would cost €20 per day to park at Piazzale Roma, and he wouldn't be using the car until next weekend. He was emphatic that it was essential to move the car before those *ladri* – robbers – charged him more money. "Come with me, we'll go bowling, park the car, and take the bus back to Venice."

It was clear that Francesco needed a break from the nonstop activity at his bar and wanted a companion. I, on the other hand, wanted nothing more than a good night's rest. But I had not yet properly greeted my friend since arriving, and it was no use arguing, especially since my Italian was not sufficient to recount the events of the previous night. I agreed to meet him, and as I left the apartment, I heard the San Giacomo dell'Orio church bells toll nine o'clock.

In a city of water with no streets to drive on, it may seem odd that parking would be a problem. While few Venetian residents had driver's licenses, even fewer owned cars, and those that did rarely drove. Perhaps this was why I would see Italian drivers shaking their fists at other drivers and yelling, "You drive like a Venetian." Driving skills aside, parking was a challenge, especially for residents of Venice.

There was a parking garage at the edge of town just off of Piazzale Roma where visitors to Venice could park before transferring to a boat or walking into town. However, most residents who owned a car had to park it on the mainland, as they couldn't afford the roughly €7000 a year to park in the island's short-term parking garage. Many used the home of a friend or relative who, in exchange, were allowed access to the car.

Italians in general paid little attention to traffic signals, road signs, or solid lines painted on the road. Venetians, however, were far worse. They drove so rarely, that it seemed each time they started over as a novice driver. As we drove on the only bridge to the mainland, it occurred to me that if I ever got to design an amusement park ride, it would be patterned after a ride in a car driven by a Venetian. Francesco lived up to every expectation I had of a Venetian driver as we picked up speed heading off the island. Fortunately, that meant the trip didn't last long.

When the car finally stopped somewhere in the mainland suburb of Mestre, I jumped out, glad to still be alive. As my stomach churned, I looked around to see that we were parked in front of a pizzeria. Sensing my confusion, Francesco informed me, "Ah, the bowling alley? It is down the street. We will first get a quick pizza." A normal meal in Italy could take four or five hours, so *quick* usually meant some time period less than three hours.

Just before midnight, we arrived at the bowling alley, where Francesco headed straight to the pool tables. Over the next two hours, we played game after game. He repeatedly explained the rules, which seemed very different from those I had learned in America. As best as I could understand it, my job was to hit some ball, but not necessarily the white one, and then wait for Francesco to hit all other the balls into the pockets, after which he would set up the table to play again. After pool, we played darts, and then finally bowled. At four o'clock, we headed to the parking lot.

Francesco dropped the car off at someone's garage, then we walked to the bus stop to catch a bus back to Venice. "Francesco," I said pointing to the bus schedule, "it's only four thirty in the morning, and the sign says that the buses don't start running until five thirty."

"Ah, back to the bowling alley then," he said, gesturing toward where we had left the car. I begged, "Please, Francesco, no more bowling!"

Laughing, he reassured me. "No more bowling. I saw my brother in the parking lot. He will drive us back to Venice." After walking back to the garage, retrieving the car, and driving back to the bowling alley, we pulled up next to Francesco's brother, who was indeed sitting by himself in the parking lot at five in the morning. Why? I had no idea.

We returned to drop off Francesco's car once again before making a stop at a café, then enduring another terrifying ride back to Piazzale Roma with his brother. It was six fifteen in the morning, and the first bus we hadn't waited for had already come and gone.

Not confident that I could even make it home without falling asleep, I went straight to a nearby café and ordered a double espresso. I thought about all of my friends whom

I had not yet properly greeted and decided it was going to be a long year.

The following morning, having finally gotten some desperately needed rest, I headed back to Mail Boxes Etc. to see what mail had accumulated since April. Strolling down *Strada Nova*, I wondered who might have sent us a card with well wishes for our year in Italy. I rounded my final corner only to be greeted by a shuttered storefront covered in cobwebs. Along with a faded Easter decoration in the window, there were dozens of old stickers on the door from overnight services announcing pending deliveries.

"I have not seen him for three months or so," the man in the adjacent furniture store informed me. "Maybe he is on a long vacation."

In this city, which was formed twelve hundred years before my own, where palaces have been owned by the same family for five hundred years, where some people work in the same jobs their entire lives, I had managed to entrust my mail to the one fly-by-night operator in town, Cesare.

I stopped in at the *enoteca*—café/wine store—on *Rio Terá Farsetti* to ask my Venetian friends if they knew anything about Cesare's whereabouts. But as I entered, I noticed a new set of faces behind the bar. My friends had sold the bar to Chinese immigrants. The new owners were very friendly, but spoke little Italian, and knew nothing about Cesare.

Determined to stay in good spirits, I decided I needed a drink. I ordered my favorite, a bottle of *Grappa di Fragoline*. An extraordinarily smooth type of Italian moonshine, the only place we had ever found it in Venice was in this store.

"L'enoteca non esista piu." Sorry, but we no longer sell wine, the new owner informed me. Dejected, I left to continue hunting for Cesare, who had disappeared without a trace.

That evening, no sooner did I sit down to write my friends and family and notify them of our new address, than one of the light bulbs in the kitchen blew out with enough force to trip the circuit breaker. I remembered seeing the panel, and located it in the dark with minimal damage to my toes. Fortunately, finding the problem circuit was no problem, even without a light, since there was only one breaker. One circuit breaker! I wondered how anyone would ever be able to isolate a problem with only one circuit for the entire apartment. And how could one breaker provide enough power for everything? A silly question I decided, since clearly, it couldn't.

The following week, Debbie, our daughter Stephanie, and the animals were scheduled to arrive. When I called to check on the moving process, I could hear the rain pounding the house back in Florida.

"Honey, you are not going to believe this!" Debbie sounded frantic, her nerves obviously strained. "There's another damn hurricane comin' right at us!" Hurricane Jeanne was expected to be the fourth named storm to make landfall in Florida. The previous two, Hurricane Charley and Hurricane Frances, had largely avoided the Tampa area, but Ivan had come very close, and Jeanne was projected to hit the bay area dead on.

When purchasing Debbie's plane ticket months ago, we discovered that she could not fly from Tampa to Venice in September due to the temperature. There are strict regulations on animal travel to prevent them from collapsing from heat exhaustion on the tarmac while waiting to be loaded or unloaded from the planes. While Venice was predicted to be cool enough, Tampa wasn't. The closest city cool enough to accept dogs was Atlanta, seven hours north of Tampa. Debbie's cat, Alexandria, would travel in the cabin.

"I'm sorry, you can't fly from Atlanta to Venice on that day," the Delta reservation agent had said of Debbie's preferred date. "There is only one flight and a maximum of two animals allowed in the cabin. There are already two animals with reservations."

They finally settled on a flight two days later that Debbie, Stephanie, and the animals would fly to Venice. "Don't worry about it," I had said at the time. "What difference could two days possibly make?" Months later, as my family tried to leave Florida in the middle of hurricane season, it seemed those two extra days in the state could prove catastrophic.

While they drove from Tampa to Atlanta, I watched the path of Hurricane Jeanne on the web. The hurricane passed from the Atlantic Ocean through south Florida, very briefly headed into the Gulf of Mexico, then turned back towards Georgia, toward Debbie, Stephanie, and the animals!

Debbie managed to call me just before her plane took off. "Barry, if we make it, we'll be the last plane out before the hurricane hits." I could hear people in the background shrieking. "The plane's shaking all over the place, and we haven't even left the gate!" Her voice trembled. I reassured her that they probably wouldn't take off unless they were certain it was perfectly safe.

I felt a huge sense of relief the following morning at Venice's Marco Polo airport as the monitor announced their flight's arrival. Shaken both literally and emotionally, Debbie and Stephanie met me with, miraculously, all twelve of their suitcases.

"So the customs authorities were happy with the animals' paperwork?" I asked, picking up the carrier that held Freckles, the heavier of our two pets.

"What authorities?" Debbie rolled her eyes. "No one even asked about any paperwork for the animals." Better safe than sorry, yes, but our transition to Venice seemed to be characterized so far by huge amounts of stress over completely unfounded concerns.

"Two thousand dollars and three months of delays for no reason at all." Debbie shook her head in disgust and glared at the airport where she had just coasted through customs.

"Benvenuto in Italia," I countered cheerfully, glad to have the ordeal over and my wife by my side. "Welcome to Italy, Debbie." She smiled and gave me a kiss. *Welcome to Italy*, I repeated to myself, *this time for a whole year.*

We made our way to the dock where the captain of the water taxi loaded the bags and animals onto his boat, then assisted each of us with a steady hand to board. As we pushed off for Venice, the water was calm, and the morning sun warmed our skin when the occasional spray sprinkled us from the bow. The smile on Debbie's face as we approached the island made it clear that the months of paperwork, planning, and packing had been worthwhile.

I was relieved that Debbie seemed pleased with the apartment I had selected. After a long day of flying, unpacking, and arranging the apartment, the sun was setting, and all was well with our world. Exhausted, Debbie went to take a shower. I peeked into the bathroom as she dried off standing in front of the sink in a puddle of water.

"Our landlord, La Signora Simonetta, has promised to install a shower curtain for us," I assured her. Debbie seemed satisfied as she wrapped herself in the towel and fumbled with the power adaptor for her hair dryer.

A moment later, Debbie turned the hair dryer to its highest setting. A loud pop came from the breaker box, and the apartment plunged into darkness.

I fumbled in the dark again to find the breaker box, flipped the power back on, and determined to buy a flashlight the next day.

We finished dinner and retired to bed early. The night gondolier poled by promptly at eleven. "What's that music?" Stephanie yelled from the small couch in the living room. Debbie groaned against her pillow. Grinning in the darkness, I yelled back, "It's Dean Martin!"

Debbie groaned again and pounded her pillow. Struggling to conceal my amusement, I cheerfully wished her, *"Buona notte,"* before rolling over and falling asleep. "Good night to you, too," she said, clearly exhausted from the trip.

I set out the next morning following my landlady's directions to what she had described as *il negozio elettrodomestici,* roughly translated an electronics store, one of just three in Venice. There, I could find anything that required batteries or had a power cord attached to it. Upon entering the store, I immediately realized that I would be able to find many of the items Debbie was still looking for. I collected several boxes, among them a small food processor, a blender and, of course, a flashlight. When I set them on the counter near the front of the store, the owner of the store greeted me and proceeded to take the blender out of the box, carefully unpacking each of the pieces and putting them together. I attempted to explain that it was unnecessary, as I would do it at home. Naturally, he paid no attention to my protests, unrolled the cord, plugged the empty blender into a power strip, and turned it on high.

"You see," he yelled over the noise, "It works. *Perfetto.*" Satisfied that the blender was in good working order, he unpacked the other items one at a time and proudly demonstrated that they also functioned as intended. He wasn't going to let anyone buy a clunker, not in his store.

Amazed, I stood and watched, imagining the furious customers in line if this were standard practice in America. Finally, he reached under the counter for some batteries, which he clearly intended to put in the flashlight. As he opened the package, I assured him that I already had plenty of batteries and was positive his flashlight would work. No, he insisted, I needed to see it work.

After he shined the flashlight in my eyes, he helped me to pile my now unpacked purchases into my *carello*. I paid for my new gadgets, along with the extra pack of batteries, and headed back to the apartment. I was fairly confident that if anything failed to work once I got home, it would be my fault, and any sort of return would be out of the question.

We quickly settled into a routine. Our days often began at a bustling courtyard, or *campo*. Our favorite was Campo San Giacomo dell'Orio, the perfect place to observe daily Venetian life. The church bells would ring, and the children played soccer against the church walls while dogs and birds drank together from the fountain. Freckles made new friends with the Venetian dogs, even though they spoke a different language. Young mothers pushed babies in strollers, while old men and women sat on benches and watched the people go by. At the edge of the square were a few popular bars where college students gathered and drank wine.

Looking around the courtyard, I saw a cat sitting in the window watching the daily parade and seeming to enjoy the diversion from household domestication. An older woman sat on a terrace full of violets looking down as if searching for someone gone long ago. Adding to the charm of the city were endless strings of quaint clotheslines, full of clothes billowing in the wind like colorful sails.

Around the corner from the campo was the pizzeria, Il Refolo. Owned by relatives of the owners of the famous Venetian restaurant Osteria Da Fiore, Il Refolo served high-quality pizza and other items in a covered patio next to a quiet canal far from the throngs of tourists at the Rialto and Saint Mark's Square. It was there in that campo that during our first September days together in Venice, Debbie and I discussed the future.

We had agreed to limit our stay to twelve months. We had both children and parents back in the States, and it seemed only reasonable to return to them after a year. In addition, I had promised the company I had helped to start twenty years earlier that I would return to work in the office after my grand telecommuting experiment.

Both Debbie and I would attend Italian classes at Istituto Venezia. Classes were every morning from nine until one o'clock and would begin in a few weeks.

My appreciation of learning a foreign language began many years ago when, at twenty-two years old, I moved to Paris on a whim. In 1979, France was in the midst of tremendous social upheaval, and I immediately enrolled in French classes just so I would know what everyone was yelling about as they marched through the streets waving signs. It wasn't long before I could make out the gist of their complaints and, soon afterward, I could distinguish which characters in the news were on each side of the debate. For weeks, I had watched the French TV station, TG1, discussing a nuclear disaster in a place called Tremil, Iceland. Later, in speaking with friends back in the States, I learned that the disaster was at Three Mile Island, but the announcer's accent was so strong I couldn't understand what he was saying.

It was with all this in mind that I had arranged for us to attend Italian classes. If we were truly to become a part of the local community, we would need a much better command of the language. For my part, I had begun listening to Italian lessons in the car to and from the office during our months of preparation back in the U.S. As a result, my vocabulary was larger than Debbie's, but my grasp of verb tenses and any remotely technical terminology was still very limited.

In the afternoons, I would work on my computer from our apartment. Debbie would visit the butcher, bakery, deli, soap store, and grocery store, and walk the dog, hang the clothes out the window to dry, and otherwise enjoy life as one of the *real housewives of Venice*. She was also looking forward to cooking with ingredients from the local market—both for us and for our Venetian friends who, during previous month-long stays in Venice, always seemed to drop by at dinnertime.

Our plan was, after Italian lessons were over for the day, we would return through the maze of alleys, stopping for groceries on the way, or so we thought. We were reminded during our first few days that all of the shops would be closed from twelve or twelve thirty until three or three thirty for lunch and the afternoon nap. So, we adjusted our schedule; Debbie would shop for the next day's meals in the evening, while I stayed at home and worked.

Despite our many habits that were incompatible with our new environment, we finally began adjusting to the fresh routines of Venice. We also began to collect more furniture and some of the household items that made us feel at home.

4

THE PRETENDERS

In our first few months of living with a new language and culture, the hardest part of communicating with the people around us was our pride. We found ourselves pointing, gesturing, and holding up a map while nodding or shaking our heads. The few words we knew were hard to pronounce correctly, so out of fear of embarrassment, we didn't even try.

The guidebooks didn't help, making claims like "You don't need to know how to speak Italian" or "Everyone speaks English." At the most basic level, for example, if you were a weekend tourist, it was true. You could survive without saying much and get by ordering in many restaurants without much knowledge of the local language. Service workers were trained in at least the basics of the "traveler's English." Simple phrases, such as "Where is the bathroom?", "Two nights for two people," and "Three scoops of vanilla ice cream, please" were generally understood. Of course, when they did respond, we didn't understand their answers anyway. In Italy at least, locals had learned to be patient, for the most part, as American visitors repeated their requests over and over, each time louder and more slowly, as though that would make English immediately more understandable.

When attempting to buy maple syrup, I drew a picture of a tree with a cup next to one of the branches. "*Sciroppo?*" the shopkeeper guessed. "*Sciroppo d'acero?*" he continued the guessing game. "No, we don't have it."

Our first weeks in Venice were filled with frustrating encounters in stores while trying to buy items such as a sifter, flyswatter, yeast, food processor, corn starch, duct tape, and American size letter paper—8.3 x 11.7 was the closest. Such items were difficult, or in some cases impossible to find, and the words we knew them by were not in the typical shopkeeper's English vocabulary. It was humbling, tiring, and more than a little disheartening to come home empty-handed after playing an hour-long game of charades with a store clerk.

To truly become Venetians, it was clear we would need a much broader vocabulary. My own Italian had matured enough that I could converse with my neighbors about many everyday topics—the weather, the high water forecast, and the *vaporetto* delays, so long as it was in the present tense. Debbie was learning, too, but we both had a long way to go.

So I wasn't surprised that during our second week in Venice as we shopped at the Coop supermarket, Debbie reached for the grape juice on the top shelf without asking for assistance from anyone at the store. As she grabbed the juice, the wrapping caught on a case of tomato juice, six bottles of which came crashing down. As the bottles hit her head and then the floor, tomato juice splattered everywhere.

Shopping a few aisles away, I cringed at the sound before rushing around the corner to find Debbie covered head to toe with juice from some of the best tasting San Marzano tomatoes in Italy! Still in shock, and very embarrassed, we tried to apologize as several Coop employees came to help. The young men assured her that it was okay while the older local women tiptoed around the mess and stared at us with disapproving looks.

Arriving back at our apartment, Debbie cried as soon as the door closed. "I was so embarrassed," she cried, tears mixing with streaks of tomato juice. "Why does everything have to be so hard?" She seemed to be feeling better as we finished putting away the groceries. "At least I found the grape juice I needed for my recipe," she sighed. "I'm going to take a shower."

I waited until I heard the water running to peek in the cabinet. The label on the purple bottle clearly read in bold script, *Succo di Mirtilli*—blueberry juice! Discussing the meaning of *mirtillo* could wait until our Italian classes began the following week.

Noting a chill in the air, I plugged in the space heater and decided to make some hot cocoa so Debbie and I could relax. A mere second after pressing the start button on the microwave, I heard a familiar pop and found myself standing in the dark again.

Shaking my head, I stood in the kitchen until I heard Debbie yelling from the shower, "Damn it! I can't see a thing." I felt around the kitchen for the flashlight without any success. I finally stumbled across the apartment and unplugged the heater before flipping the breaker back on.

As I settled back into my chair with the flashlight on the table, I heard the shower stop, and Debbie getting dressed.

The silence ended abruptly as Debbie turned on her hair dryer. Fifteen seconds later, it was quiet as the apartment plunged into darkness once again. Making my way carefully to the breaker panel, I decided the extra batteries might come in handy after all.

Thankfully, when I came to Venice to find an apartment, I chose a residential part of town: Santa Croce. The area is mostly apartments, and on our *calle* there were no late night restaurants or cafés. When the realtor and the elderly owner had shown me the ground floor apartment on a quiet canal, the allure of the neighborhood pulled me in. Our landlady, Simonetta, lived in the apartment upstairs by herself, so there would be no loud parties or fights to interrupt the peace from above. The garden had a ten-foot-high wall on the canal, so noise from the boats would be minimal. As I signed the lease, thoughts of tranquility in paradise floated through my head. Debbie had heard my description of the area on many occasions, and both of us were looking forward to a peaceful existence in Venice.

At seven o'clock in the morning, the first church bells of the day rang out. The smooth tones of the pealing bells were a pleasant way to start the day. Unfortunately, the church bells also signaled the beginning of the workday.

Crash! Bang! I jerked awake, my idyllic dreams of peace and tranquility broken. A parade of about ten construction workers showed up at the dock outside the apartment every day with the ringing of the bells. Old bricks and concrete pieces were dumped hurriedly into the boat just outside my window. Yelling and banging continued as the wheelbarrows were loaded with cement from a second boat. The parade of old men in shorts continued down the street to a building under construction. It seemed as if the workers must have been paid by the load! I had never seen or heard such a constant parade of wheelbarrows going so quickly and so noisily. Were they the only people in the city who didn't take a break for lunch?

After closing my windows, retrieving my MP3 player, and putting on my headphones, I sat back and closed my eyes with a satisfied sigh as the sounds of Vivaldi drowned out the racket. Peace and tranquility had again returned to Venice, if only in my mind.

A few days later, I was passing through Santa Croce, and noticed that Gelateria Alaska, the same shop which had been "closed due to illness" when we visited years before, was now open. The man behind the counter was over six-feet-tall, appeared to be in his early forties, and wore a white apron smeared with fruits of various colors. He was exchanging music CDs with a young man in dreadlocks. Reggae music played in the background. As the young man left, the man behind the counter turned toward me and smiled.

"*Ciao, signore. Cosa prendi?*"

Instead of answering his question of "What'll you have?" I asked, "Are you Carlo?"

"That is me, Carlo Pistacchi," he said in a proud voice.

"Welcome back," I replied. "My name is Giuseppe Frangipane." I knew better by this time than to try and explain the name Barry. "My wife Deborah heard many years ago that you have the best gelato in Venice, but you were sick when we came to visit."

Carlo assured me he had made a full return to good health and thanked me for my concern. He explained that his grandfather was a gelato maker, and that because his last name—*Pistacchi*—means pistachio, he was destined for the business of gelato.

"Try the pistachio." He handed me a bit of the gray-green colored confection on the tip of a spoon and waited for my reaction. The color resembled baby food, but I knew that was the mark of real pistachios. I tasted and affirmed that it was in fact very good.

"Delicious, no?" Carlo explained that his pistachios were flown in from Sicily, and that he used only natural and fresh ingredients. I told him that the color was a dead giveaway of the quality. The bright-green pistachio gelato I had seen at many places was made with a powder mix and food coloring. Carlo was thrilled to find someone who appreciated the difference.

I tried his apple, pear, and cantaloupe flavors. Each displayed the true essence of its namesake as if I was eating the fruit itself. Carlo described how he made each flavor fresh from fruits he found at the market each morning. "If it's not fresh, if it's not in season, I don't use it."

Settling on the pear gelato, I thanked him and took out two euro coins to pay.

"*No, non paghi oggi.*" You don't pay today, he insisted. "I will see you again, Giuseppe. Next time bring Deborah!" As I went on my way, the reggae music fading in the distance, it was clear why so many people cared so deeply for this man. As I became more and more a part of the community, such protests of "*No, non paghi oggi*" became all too common.

A week had passed when I returned with Debbie to Gelateria Alaska, introducing her to both Carlo and the incredible flavor of his gelato. His freezer display was full of surprises: blueberry, watermelon, peach, and something called "zenzero." But Carlo was nowhere to be found.

We waited inside the store for a few minutes, then stepped outside and looked around. Another shopkeeper saw us waiting and called out toward a café several doors down. Standing in the doorway talking to the owner of the café was Carlo. Seeing us in front of his store, he waved and arrived a few minutes later after finishing his animated conversation with the café owner. Debbie noted that his strength had certainly returned, and he was energetic as he greeted us.

"Ciao, Giuseppe! And you must be Deborah!" He greeted her with a kiss on each cheek, gave me a hug, and ushered us into the store. "Today you must try my best flavor. It is *zenzero!*" He pointed to the white gelato with no clearly identifiable origin. Sensing our confusion, Carlo explained, "In English, you call it "ginger."

The first taste brought a sharp ginger flavor, immediately followed by a burning sensation, strong enough to make my eyes water. *"Santa Maria, Carlo!"* Handing me a glass of water, he explained that, like all his ingredients, the ginger was fresh and a bit strong. Laughing, he agreed that it was an acquired taste, and perhaps not for everyone.

Debbie seemed to enjoy her cup of the *zenzero*, while I settled on the peach gelato. I asked Carlo about the long hours his shop was open.

"I am open seven days a week, ten months out of the year," he explained. "It is hard work, but I meet new friends every day, and then I enjoy my time off."

As I reached for my money to pay, Carlo smiled and told me, "One euro. Only for yours, nothing for Deborah's." Ignoring his offer, I put two euro on the counter, and we ran out the door ignoring Carlo's shout of "Giuseppe, you paid me too much!"

Do You Like Fish?

The following week, Debbie told me she had offered our help to Francesco for a gardening project. Francesco's little *Bar ai Miracoli*—in Venice most bars were also cafés—was just outside the *Chiesa dei Miracoli.* The *Chiesa dei Miracoli, or* the Church of the Miracles, was a Venice landmark, old and grand, made almost entirely of marble. Legend holds that in the 1400s, a statue of the Virgin Mary on its lot was responsible for a number of miracles in Venice. Sadly, on that day, we would not be saved by a miracle.

Francesco's design seemed simple enough. He had acquired sixteen flower boxes, intending to create an attractive, lively atmosphere in and around his café to rival the regality of the nearby church. It was September, however, and he had yet to purchase either the soil or the flowers.

Debbie had offered to plant the flowers for him, which naturally meant that we would work together. I made six trips between the nearby flower shop one bridge away lugging a twenty-five-pound bag of soil on each trip. Debbie followed carrying trays of pansies. For the remainder of the day, we sat on the ground filling the flower boxes with dirt, eventually planting over a hundred pansies.

Tired, I stood back and admired the view. As Debbie leaned over the canal to fill her bucket with water for the flowers, a passing tourist commented in English, "Oh, how pretty! I just love the way Venetians work hard to keep everything so nice with all the flowers!" Debbie and I, covered with soil, beamed with pride.

Francesco was also pleased with the flowers, which made his bar look warm and inviting. In fact, he was so happy that he offered to take us out to dinner. "My cousin has a fish restaurant," he told us excitedly. "Do you like fish?"

Debbie and I looked at each other with smiles. *Real Italian seafood!* We gladly took him up on his offer and, after a well-deserved shower, returned to meet Francesco.

The restaurant was cozy and unpretentious, with just a few tables seating locals. The first dish was calamari. While not our favorite, we did manage to get down the somewhat chewy pieces of fried squid while looking forward to what most certainly would be coming next. Perhaps we would enjoy a nice tuna filet, or possibly a beautiful piece of sea bass.

The next course was large plates of seafood pasta. By seafood, I mean a collection of virtually everything that they could find in the Venetian lagoon. Steamed octopus with eyes staring up as if to say, "Why me?" was mixed with chopped squid and fresh spaghetti. Atop the mix was perched a bizarre creature. no doubt some sort of rare delicacy, that resembled a kind of large seafaring cockroach.

"Oh, I'm so full already!" Debbie exclaimed as I stared at my dish. It was clear from her expression that she would rather starve than eat what was staring back at her from the plate. Francesco looked disappointed at first, but then brightened. "No problem! Barry, we will share Debbie's plate," he announced helpfully, pulling the plate of seafood pasta toward me. Gee, why didn't I think of that? I forced a half-hearted smile before glaring at my wife. Debbie was thoroughly tickled at my extra helping of creatures from the Venetian lagoon. As I picked at my plate, I could still see her smirk out of the corner of my eye.

"Barry! Debbie! This is my way to thank you," Francesco voiced his appreciation. I assured him that, yes, he really had thanked us enough already, and that any more seafood would be entirely more thanks than we deserved. Ignoring my protests, he confirmed with his cousin that another course was on its way, leaving me to wonder what the next surprise might be.

Thankfully, the fish lasagna that soon arrived would mark the end of our meal. Debbie, having already proclaimed herself full, was exempted from yet another aquatic masterpiece. She seemed perfectly content to watch in amusement as I forced down the last few bites.

The next morning, she teased me, asking innocently, "Are you okay? You look a little green." I informed her that if she was going to plant any more flowers, she would have to do it alone. My stomach couldn't handle another thank you.

Acqua Alta

Acqua Alta, the infamous high water of Venice, has been a fact of life for locals for over a millennium. The frequency and intensity of the floods increased gradually with each year. Weather played its part in late fall and winter as a combination of heavy rains and high tides brought an influx of water. The *sirocco* winds blew in a northerly direction, trapping the tides in the lagoon. Venice has been sinking at a rate of roughly one inch every ten years since measurements began in 1897. *Acqua Alta* was now so frequent and severe that the ground floors of most of the palaces, or *palazzi*, on the Grand Canal had been permanently vacated.

Piazza San Marco—Saint Mark's Square—was located in one of the city's lowest areas, and thus flooded first. The pictures of Venice during *Acqua Alta* always looked so romantic. The newspapers showed Julia Roberts smiling as she waded through knee-deep water in *Piazza San Marco,* or tourists standing on the folding tables used as raised walkways in some parts of the city. Debbie and I had spent enough time in the city to know that, in reality, the flooding made daily life a challenge in the winter months.

It was about eight o'clock on the morning of October 31, when the high-water sirens sounded for the first time during our stay. Residents knew the sirens offered two hours' warning before the water reached 100 centimeters, the level where it would begin to flood the land. There were a few areas, such as *Piazza San Marco*, that were affected at 90cm. At 130cm, seventy percent of the walkways were under water; at 140cm, almost all of the walkways were submerged. It was two hours later when we lost power in our ground floor apartment. Flipping the breaker proved fruitless; it immediately tripped again as soon as it was turned on.

The water had already risen to 110cm, the level at which it had been predicted to crest an hour later. Although we already had about five inches of water in the alley outside our front door, I decided to go for a walk in my high-water boots and find some lunch. Debbie thought it best to stay home with the animals.

As I made my way through town, the water continued to rise, and there were many places where my eighteen-inch boots were not sufficient. Though my feet were soaked and cold, I pressed on. The electronic displays scattered throughout the city to indicate the high-water forecast still showed a maximum of 110cm, but it was clear to anyone outside that the water would exceed that level. I sloshed along, taking note of the different ways that people dealt with *Acqua Alta*. Groups of tourists were stranded in the center of the small squares known as *campi* with water rising around them as they tried to keep their tennis shoes dry. Some had resorted to encasing their legs in plastic garbage bags and sloshing through the city; others took off their shoes and walked barefoot through the flooded *calli*. Shopkeepers, well-prepared with hip boots, typically stood outside their stores talking to one another as the water continued to rise. Many stayed closed, no doubt hoping to prevent additional damage to the merchandise by waves caused by the customers wading through the store. The popular pizzeria, *Ae Oche*, although flooded as much as all the other shops, continued to serve pizza in to-go boxes to wading passers-by.

I poked my head into *Bagalo*, the small bar in *Campo San Giacomo dell'Orio*. Everything was business as usual, except for a few almost comical differences. Four tourists stood in bare feet with their pants rolled up to the knee. The two dogs relaxing inside were dry, having apparently been carried into the bar by their owners. There seemed to be more locals than usual, no doubt taking advantage of this break in their ordinary routine. Whether in bare feet or high-water boots, everyone was enjoying wine or hot chocolate in the knee-deep water. A few stood at the bar, while others kept their feet propped up on stools and tall chairs.

Continuing down the street to Pizza 2000, I joined a group to help hoist the Coke machine onto six large cans of tomatoes to raise it up out of the water. The man in the realtor's office next door was busy placing his computers on top of the desks. The water was well above the predicted mark.

I arrived at *Pasticceria Il Bucintoro*, our friend Gino's pastry shop, to find that it was closed for the day. Who could blame him? As I stood in eighteen inches of water deciding where to go for lunch, several tourists waded by. They asked a group of shopkeepers for directions to *Piazza San Marco*.

"Can you swim?" The men laughed. I explained to the visitors that the water was waist deep in *Piazza San Marco*. I gave them directions, but advised against going there with the water at its current level. They thanked me, but chose to trudge ahead toward their destination with plastic bags covering their legs. Tourists. Although to be fair, unlike them, I could go to the *Piazza* any day.

Shortly after noon, I called Debbie to explain that the water was now at 137cm and that I would wait for it to recede before heading back. She begged me to come home as soon as possible.

"The power is still off, and I can't get it to come back on."

Since it was impossible to return home without a boat, I decided it was time to find lunch and a place to sit. Back at *Bagalo*, the locals were discussing the *sirocco* winds. "The tides we can predict," one shopkeeper said with a shrug. "The *sirocco*? That is another story."

"When MOSE is finished, it will help," the bartender offered.

"Finished?" A chorus of objections and arguments erupted about the controversial project. Begun fifteen years before, MOSE, *Modulo Sperimentale Elettromeccanico*, was an experimental design that consisted of seventy-eight underwater gates designed to reduce the intensity of *Acqua Alta* by closing off the Venetian lagoon, thus protecting Venice from the constant damage from the floods. Without MOSE or some other sort of protection, Venice could become uninhabitable in less than a hundred years. Public skepticism about the project was understandable given the snail's pace at which progress had been made. Constant appeals were made by various constituencies, resulting in a series of alternate proposals being presented and evaluated. Meanwhile, Venetians would simply put on their high-water boots and wade out to run their errands, just like on any other day.

As the water had started to recede, and all the pastries at *Bagalo* had been eaten, I stopped at the Coop supermarket on the way home. Customers pushed their carts full of groceries through two inches of water, leaving small wakes behind them. The store was busy, as the following day would be All-Saints day, and most stores would be closed.

I sloshed my way home, grocery bags slung over my shoulder as I thought about the tourists laughing while they were walking through the water barefoot, carefree and on vacation. I looked down to see a drowned rat float by my boots. As I drew closer to the house, another rat floated by, as did a dead mouse.

With the water receding, power to the apartment had been restored, and life returned to what we would come to call "normal" in a city that practically floats on the water. Debbie informed me that the *Acqua Alta* forecast for the following day was ten centimeters higher than the forecast had been for today. Fortunately, the forecast was incorrect again, and the *Acqua Alta* stopped at a manageable level.

The Electricians – Certainly Only Part 1

It didn't escape my notice that the problem of the stubborn circuit breaker coincided directly with the arrival of *Acqua Alta* on Sunday. There were no other obvious causes that would explain the problem, since there was no rain, and we hadn't used any of the power-hungry appliances typically responsible for overloading the apartment's one circuit. Time and again, Debbie went into the foyer to reset the breaker, but it continued to trip immediately back into the off position. We unplugged everything in the apartment, but still the breaker wouldn't reset. Exasperated, Debbie went upstairs to speak with our landlady. She returned a few minutes later with La Signora Simonetta.

"I do not know how this could it be," she pondered. "Have you unplugged everything and tried it again?" With a loud sigh, my wife assured her that we had already tried that. I wondered to myself what good it would do to have the breaker turned on if we couldn't plug anything in. Debbie proposed that perhaps it was the *Acqua Alta*. After all, nothing else had changed other than the level of continually rising water outside. La Signora assured her that although she had encountered at least three short circuits in the apartment, she had never experienced problems due to *Acqua Alta*, since all electrical wiring was installed overhead.

La Signora left to call an electrician. We waited, frustrated that Debbie's plans to spend the weekend cooking had just come to an abrupt end. Our landlady returned to explain that because it was Sunday morning, and Monday was a holiday, the electrician and his partner would not be available until Tuesday morning. Debbie agreed that would be okay as long as we could find a place to put all of the meats and other groceries she had just purchased. Later that afternoon, after the water receded substantially, we found that the circuit breaker could finally be reset, and the power restored. Surely this correlation would be enough to convince the electricians that the root of the problem lay with *Acqua Alta*.

On Tuesday morning, the electrician and his assistant arrived as promised. I carefully explained how the power went off as the water rose and came back on when the water receded, noting the timing of the problem's arrival and departure. After listening intently, the electrician placed his hand on my shoulder and assured me earnestly that all of the wiring was overhead, and that the *Acqua Alta* couldn't possibly have anything to do with the problem.

The two of them went into the garden. "There it is," the senior electrician said pointing confidently. "It is this light on the outside wall."

Confused as to what evidence was there to support his conclusion, I protested, "It's six feet off of the ground and wasn't even on. How could that possibly cause the problem?" He explained patiently that there must be a short in the light caused when it would rain, and that when the wire dried out, the short disappeared. The junior electrician nodded sagely in agreement.

"But it wasn't raining on Sunday," I argued. Besides, when it had rained for days the previous week, the problem hadn't occurred. But it was no use. He had found the problem.

"You will see; you will see," he promised. He explained that he was the one who had rewired the entire apartment earlier in the year, and that the only thing he had not rewired was the lighting in the garden. It was unbelievable, yet suddenly clear. His process of elimination left only the poor old wall light fixture outside to be blamed.

They set to work on the light fixture and, a short while later, announced that their work was complete. "All finished. You see, everything works. *Perfetto.*" Proud to have solved the problem, he closed the lid of his toolbox vigorously.

I couldn't believe my ears. Everything had already been working when he had arrived, clearly because the water had receded. What would happen with the next *Acqua Alta*?

He explained that he had simply clipped the wire right at the point where the old wiring met his new wiring. "*Non ti preoccupare!* That old lamp will not cause you any more trouble," he reassured me. Of course, with the wires clipped, the lamp wouldn't be providing us with light either.

The men reentered the apartment, where they made their way to the bathroom. "La Signora tells me that you need a shower curtain," the electrician informed me as he measured feverishly around the shower.

"I see. You are not only an electrician," I inquired, "but you also install shower curtains?" Hiding my doubts about his skillset was becoming ever more difficult.

"It is true I am also a plumber," he answered with a broad grin, stepping out of the bathroom. "I will be back in the afternoon with a shower curtain." Not only was I surprised by his sudden punctuality, I wondered whether I should allow him to touch anything else in the apartment.

Sensing my hesitation, Debbie joined the conversation. "We do need a shower curtain," she pleaded.

"Well then, we will see you this afternoon." I sighed.

"Oh no," he looked mildly horrified, and his assistant shook his head vigorously. "I am far too busy today. But when I come back, it will be in the afternoon," he assured me.

Debbie and I just stared at each other in wide-eyed amazement. After they left, I wondered aloud to Debbie whether his final solution to our problem of getting water on the bathroom floor might be to cut off the water to the showerhead. "That old shower won't cause you any more trouble," I imitated wagging my finger. Debbie chuckled before collapsing on the bed with a groan.

We stayed in that apartment for four more months. The electrician/plumber never returned, not in the afternoon, nor in the morning, not ever. But then again, *Acqua Alta* never caused another power failure, either.

Going to School

Acqua Alta and our electrical adventures behind us, Debbie and I were now comfortable in our daily routine. Each morning, we left the apartment in Santa Croce at eight o'clock, walked to Rosetta's café in *Campo de le Strope,* and had our morning brioche, pain au chocolat, and coffee. We would walk by the residential canal of *Rio Marin* with private boats docked in front of each home, the gothic church build in the 1300s which the locals call the *Frari,* the lively *Campo Santa Margherita,* typically full of students from the nearby university, and finally arrive at our Italian school, *Istituto Venezia* in *Campo San Barnaba,* just a few steps away from the boat selling fresh produce by the *Ponte dei Pugni,* or Bridge of Fists. The *Ponte dei Pugni* is so named because in the 1600s, different factions in the city would fight on the bridge. There were no guardrails on the bridges back then, and the fight would end when one, or both, of the fighters ended up in the water. Marble footprints on the top of the bridge marked the spot where the dueling parties would place their feet, waiting for the call to start fighting.

Over time, we learned what all Venetians already knew—traveling the back alleys made it possible to avoid the mass of tourists that swarmed in certain parts of the city each day.

The other students in our class were from all over the world—Peru, Germany, Sweden, Mexico, Japan, France, and other countries—and few of them spoke any English. All of the lectures were in Italian, but over time, we began to learn more and more. Debbie now understood, for instance, how to order a *caffe corretto con grappa* during our ten-minute break each morning. In typical Italian logic, this meant that her coffee was *corretto,* or corrected, with a shot of *grappa.* I was curious why the Italians would feel their coffee needed correction. At eleven o'clock, we would run from the school to the café Imagina around the corner and get a coffee and *tramezzino,* a sandwich of white bread filled with tuna, olives, hard-boiled eggs, ham, prosciutto, and cheese. All the students stood around the bar downing their espresso and sandwiches, since the short break didn't provide enough time for table service. We would always rush to return to class before our ten minutes had passed and were frequently late, sneaking in quietly, two adults behaving like schoolchildren.

Each day at one o'clock, the school secretary traversed the halls ringing a bell to announce the end of class. The walk home was a quiet one since the grocery stores, hardware shops, pharmacies, and banks were all closed at that time. But there was always the pizzeria in *Campo Santa Margherita* for a slice of pizza along the way. In the afternoons, I worked on computer programs while Debbie studied Italian and prepared dinner.

Italian Crepes

Each day on the way to school, we would pass a restaurant supply store in San Polo, where a large crepe machine sat in the window. While not Italian, crepes were still one of my favorite foods. Just seeing the machine each morning was enough to make me envision tasting the warm dough filled with butter and sugar, chocolate Grand Marnier, egg and Gruyere, or banana and chocolate. It was a complete stand, about a meter wide by a meter tall. The crepe griddle sat on one side, with a covered storage counter for the Nutella, fruit, and sugar on the other.

For weeks, I dreamed someone would buy the stand so I could have some warm fresh crepes. One day, on our way to school, the crepe stand was gone. I rubbed my hands together in anticipation. Debbie wondered how we would find out who had bought it. I assured her that I would find out.

Sure enough, a few days later the crepe stand appeared with its new owner outside a local café. Excited, I asked the friendly elderly lady for a butter and sugar crepe and waited, visions of the perfect French crepe floating in my head. The combination of rich creamy butter mixing with the melted sugar on a thin golden crepe was a treat well worth waiting for.

My excitement quickly turned to concern, however, as the lady turned the griddle on and poured cold batter onto a still cold griddle. After waiting a minute or so for it to warm up, I watched in horror as she added some cold butter and sugar to the raw batter and proceeded to fold it into a blob that resembled a large meatball. My heart sank as she proudly wrapped the mushy, raw concoction in wax paper, handed it to me, and smiled. Not wanting to hurt her feelings, I waited until I was around the corner before throwing the batter into the nearest garbage can.

A week later, the crepe stand had returned to the restaurant supply store. Debbie giggled as I gazed at it again with a distant look. It seemed that Italians should stick to making prosciutto and pasta, and leave the crepe making to the French.

Almost Knowing the Language

After a month of classes, Debbie and I were becoming more confident in our ability to converse in Italian. We met our friend Gino at his *pasticceria* on our way home from school. We discovered he made some of the best pastries in Venice, but like so many other Italians, he found it impossible to pronounce my first name. And like so many of our Venetian friends, he took to calling me Giuseppe.

"Giuseppe, *il mio grande amico!*" As we entered his shop one day, Gino asked me for a small favor. Pointing to the sign in his window, he inquired whether his English translation was correct. His cousin had translated it for him, and it now listed German and English variations in addition to the Italian. Well, sort of. The English text on the sign read, "It only knows it and for service to table." I had to read it a few times and refer to the Italian before realizing what he meant. In the cafés of Italy and elsewhere in Europe, there were two prices, one if you ate or drank standing up, and another, higher price if you have table service. The owner paid the wait staff out of the higher sitting price, and tipping was largely superfluous. Of course, many tourists were unaware of that and would order and pay for coffee and pastries while standing, and then sit down at the table to eat. Because cafés were typically small, table space was precious, so that cheated the waiter or waitress. While the price difference could be as much as triple for table service, in most establishments, it served as "rent" for as long as you wished to use the table. It was not uncommon for guests to spend an hour or two for the price of one cappuccino.

Gino's hope for his new sign was to communicate succinctly to patrons that the dining room was for table service only. I explained with a chuckle that perhaps a slight rephrasing would help. "The tables are for waiter service only," I wrote on a napkin for him. A week later, the new sign appeared.

"*Giuseppe, il mio grande amico?*" Gino asked me again, proudly showing off his new sign. Much better, I congratulated him, wondering silently what the German translation really said. In any case, I was pleased that my Italian was now good enough to be of assistance.

As Debbie and I sat finishing our pastries, we performed our daily routine, attempting to read the local newspaper, *Il Gazzettino,* and comprehend some subset of the stories it contained. We labored over an article about a train wreck that had occurred somewhere in Italy.

Unable to discern exactly what the cause of the wreck had been, I decided to cheat, opening my laptop to decipher a difficult sentence using a translation website. I first found the article online, and then copied and pasted the text into the translator, which promptly returned a less-than-eloquent English sentence.

Trenitalia asserts that the train left from Palermo centers them to the 12,10 and directed to Raisi Tip non it is derailed but has blinked against a paraurti. According to Trenitalia, beyond to the hurt machinist, there would be six persons contuse.

No less confused than before, I concluded that continuing to attend class was a far superior option than using technology. I would have to live without knowing what caused the train wreck.

Just for fun, I typed in the Italian version of Gino's sign, *"La sala e solo per servizio a tavola."* The program returned with *"It only knows it and for service to table."* I knew where Gino's cousin had learned English.

Electric Blankets

Zia Lina, my grandmother's sister, was a proud but poor woman, and didn't have a lot of heat in her small apartment in the countryside of Treviso, a half hour outside of Venice. In the wintertime, frequently the only form of heat she had was an electric blanket.

Debbie and I took a few days away from Venice and spent it at her apartment. We spent the first day listening to stories of my grandmother's childhood and eating foods prepared according to local traditions; at the end of the day, we retired to our bedroom to freeze our buns off during the night, just as they must have done years ago. The next day, we went to downtown Treviso to acquire an extra electric blanket for Zia Lina's apartment, and one for us as well.

COIN, the closest thing to a department store in Treviso, had four or five floors of clothing and home furnishings. Debbie and I admired the thick down comforters in various shades of white, but decided to stick with our original plan of getting an electric blanket. We searched every floor in the store, but found no electric blankets.

"Where are the electric blankets?" we finally asked the store clerk.

She seemed a bit shocked at the question, but replied nicely enough, "We don't sell electric blankets here. You need to go to an electric store for that." An electric store, she explained, sold mixers, blenders, razors, vacuum cleaners, light bulbs, and, of course, electric blankets.

"The store across the street has some nice ones," she told us helpfully, finding our search for an electric blanket amusing. "But of course, they are closed now because it is Wednesday morning."

"Wednesday morning?" I asked curiously, somewhat dreading the answer.

"Yes, they are open Saturday morning, so they are closed Wednesday morning." I stood there for a moment, trying to rationalize what I had heard, but quickly gave up; Italy had its own rules about hours of operation.

We went back to Zia Lina's and deferred our purchase of an electric blanket until Saturday. I was just hoping that there wasn't also an "extension cord store" where I would need to go to get an extension cord for the electric blanket. If there was, something told me that they would be closed Saturday morning, but they would, of course, be open all day on Wednesday.

5

DEATH IN VENICE

The holiday season started as a time of celebration. But before the season was over, tragedy would hit the family.

Thanksgiving

Ah, Thanksgiving! The time of year when we relaxed with our friends and reflected upon the past year while eating the traditional Thanksgiving feast. Afterward, we watched football before heading out to the malls for those great early season deals. At least in America, that was the custom; this year, we were in Italy.

We decided to host a Thanksgiving Day meal at our apartment in Venice. Having met quite a few new friends over the almost three months since our arrival, the list of guests grew to about fifteen people, as many were curious about this American holiday, referred to as the *Festa di Ringraziamento* in Italy. Debbie put together her usual list of dishes: Roast turkey, mashed potatoes with sour cream, sweet potatoes, pecan pie, pumpkin pie, and a ham roasted with cloves, pineapple, and brown sugar. Additionally, for some of our vegetarian friends, Debbie would cook macaroni and cheese and bowtie pasta in marinara sauce.

Four days before Thanksgiving, Debbie came home from the Rialto market with a twenty-pound turkey. "The butcher held them all up by the neck, and this was the biggest one," she said, pulling the turkey out of our *carello*.

I had to admit, it was a nice sized bird. "But where will we cook it? All we have is this microwave convection oven, and it's barely big enough for a chicken!"

"Well, I haven't gotten that far," Debbie huffed. "I figured you would think of something," she said, annoyed. We finally decided to ask La Signora if we could use her oven to cook the turkey. We had been in her apartment and had seen her full-sized oven.

"A nine-kilo turkey?" La Signora chuckled. "All I have is a microwave half the size of yours." She proudly showed me the inside of her oven; it was full of neatly stacked pots and pans. "The oven broke a few years ago, and since I live by myself, the microwave is sufficient." She then showed me how she used her broken dishwasher to store clean dishes, and how the broken freezer was used for paper plates, napkins, and aluminum foil.

Debbie began to wring her hands feverishly. We had a twenty-pound turkey, and no way to cook it! "Wait," I thought. "I'll just ask Davide." Davide and his wife Irene had cooked dinner for us in their apartment; certainly, they would let us use their oven!

I called Davide and told him that I had a favor to ask. He invited me over, offered me a cup of coffee, and listened to my problem. Unfortunately, Davide, like the rest of Venice, didn't have a full-size oven. "All I have is this tiny microwave oven and my two-burner stove," he gestured apologetically. "It is very tricky making a large dinner here, as everything needs to be prepared in advance and then warmed in just the right order."

He then pointed out that our mutual friend Renata owned the pizzeria just down the street; perhaps she would allow us the use of her pizza oven. The idea of using a stone hearth to cook a turkey brought forth images of Debbie pulling a flattened, charred bird out on a flat paddle. The thought of all their pizzas smelling like turkey, not to mention the half-mile walk home with a fully-dressed, hot bird, didn't seem sensible.

Ah, but Gino would have an oven! While his house was in a nearby town, like many *Veneziani,* he also has an apartment in Venice. That allowed him the opportunity to sleep in town during the week and go straight to work at the pasticceria. I went to see Gino at *Il Bucintoro*, my third stop in the hunt for an oven. Over a glass of Prosecco, I described the problem.

"I would love to help, but the oven in the apartment hasn't worked in years," Gino said apologetically. "Have you thought about cutting up the turkey and cooking it on the stove?" I had considered that option, but since Debbie had never cooked a turkey on the stove, and the presentation of the beautiful brown bird was part of the festivities, I ruled it out... for the moment, anyway.

Debbie cried when I returned and told her the news. It was two days before Thanksgiving, and we had no oven! We had invited over fifteen people to our house, and we still had no place to cook the turkey.

On the day before Thanksgiving, I stopped at our local bar for a macchiato. Rosetta and Renzo, the owners, laughed when I told them of my plight. Rosetta thought for a moment, then said, "My friend owns a local restaurant. Why don't you cook it there?" The idea of walking into a restaurant in which I had never even eaten and asking the owners to use their oven seemed a bit strange to me, but I was getting desperate. "Come back at three o'clock this afternoon, and I will go with you," Rosetta told me warmly. "I'll introduce you to the owner of the restaurant, and you can ask to use her oven." I immediately agreed to return at three, but could not help my growing feeling of discomfort.

While walking home, I stopped at our friend Renata's pizzeria. "Why do you look so down?" she asked. Again, I explained the story of the turkey and no oven. She laughed heartily. "Don't worry about asking someone else," she said. "I live just around the corner. You and Debbie can use my oven. My husband and I will be here working all day, so you can just come in and out of the house as you wish. It won't be any trouble at all." I happily agreed to her proposal and cancelled my meeting with Rosetta. It was funny how, after days of searching for an oven, the idea of cooking a twenty-pound turkey as far as three blocks, one bridge, and two flights of stairs away from the house seemed the perfect solution!

Debbie seemed thrilled when I got home and shared the news about the oven. "I only have a few problems left," she informed me in relief, pulling out a written list. "I can't find sour cream, cheddar cheese, brown sugar, pecans, sweet potatoes, cloves, corn syrup, baking soda or vanilla extract." We left the house with our cell phones, each on a mission to find the remaining ingredients. We would call each other if we found something. It would be fun, a real-life treasure hunt in Venice! I kissed her goodbye and off we went.

"I found the baking soda in the baby section of a supermarket in Piazzale Roma," Debbie texted. "The lady in the wine store told me to look in the baby department."

For my part, I had checked four or five stores for vanilla extract and had come up empty. A quick check with Gino at the pasticceria confirmed my suspicions; vanilla extract did not exist in Italy, or at least, not in Venice. There was something called "aroma di vaniglia" which could only be described as a vanilla flavoring in sugar water. After a chance meeting over a glass of wine with a friend from the States, I called Debbie. "Cecilia says we can make vanilla extract by heating a vanilla bean in pure alcohol, and I found a vanilla bean!"

The cheddar cheese was found in a small imported cheese store in the Castello neighborhood on the other side of town.

When we met back at the house, we had found brown sugar at a health food store and cane sugar syrup, which would take the place of corn syrup. Once we knew their names in Italian, the sweet potatoes, *patate americane*, and pecans, *noci California*, were easier to find.

Cloves were purchased from Màscari, the specialty store of last resort near the fish market at the Rialto Bridge. Anytime we couldn't find something in Venice, the locals would tell us to try Màscari. There, the spices were stored in drawers, then dumped out on a piece of paper in the necessary quantity. The paper was then folded, taped shut, and sold.

We returned to the apartment with everything but the sour cream. The mashed potatoes simply wouldn't be the same without sour cream, so I decided to experiment. After trying a few things, I discovered that a mixture of two parts *panna di cucina*, a very thick cream, and one part plain yogurt was almost indistinguishable from sour cream. We were ready to begin!

Exhausted, but elated from our treasure hunt, I cleaned the apartment while Debbie made the pies and the potatoes. One by one, the delicious foods were cooked in our tiny oven. At midnight, we retired to bed and discussed the plan for the next day. We would carry the turkey to Renata's apartment; then, Debbie would return every half hour to baste the turkey while cooking the ham, macaroni and cheese, and marinara sauce at home in between basting sessions.

In the morning, Debbie and I carried the turkey to Renata's apartment and placed it in the oven. My phone rang while I was making a run to the wine store. It was Debbie, crying. "I just returned to Renata's apartment to baste the turkey, and I'm standing outside in the *calle* because the key won't unlock the door." I showed up to help, but was no more successful than Debbie. Meanwhile, the turkey was cooking, or possibly burning, without basting, and we had no way of getting in. It was noon, and there would be no way Renata could leave the pizzeria to help us with the door. Nonetheless, Debbie ran to see Renata, who had a restaurant full of hungry *Veneziani*.

"Sorry, my set of keys does not work very well," Renata said, rummaging through a drawer while keeping a careful eye on the pizzas and customers. "Here's another set." Debbie ran back to the apartment, entered with ease, and checked on the turkey. It was cooking to perfection.

While I was at the market getting onions, Debbie called, again close to crying in frustration. "I'm standing outside *our* apartment now; I left the keys inside!" I closed my eyes and prayed for a return to sanity. "Oh, never mind," she added. "La Signora is home and is coming to let me in." I opened my eyes, shrugged at a curious Venetian, and paid for the onions.

The turkey was done shortly before the guests were scheduled to arrive. We hadn't considered the challenge of carrying a hot, twenty-pound turkey sitting in at least six cups of gravy back to the house. After pouring all of the gravy into a pot, we wrapped the turkey in aluminum foil and placed it in a canvas sack for the trip home.

Debbie set out her culinary masterpieces buffet style, as friends from Germany, Sweden, Spain, Japan, China, Italy, and the States arrived, many of which we had met in our Italian language classes. Prosecco seemed appropriate as we toasted the American holiday in the only language common to all those present: Italian.

Debbie and I answered their many questions about the meaning and origin of Thanksgiving. Each person at our table gave thanks, some for being fortunate enough to be spending time in Venice. Debbie and I gave thanks for the oven in our home back in America, as well as for our friends here in Venice who made this international Thanksgiving truly a day to remember.

McDebbie

We were sitting in a café near the Rialto Bridge when my phone rang. It was my aunt Loredana from Sarmede, which was about an hour north of Venice. "The year is almost over, and we would like to see you and Deborah. We are all getting together for lunch tomorrow. This year's Prosecco is especially good, and we are preparing a big feast to celebrate. Come join us." When the family invited you to lunch, it was quite an insult to decline. "Um, sure, we'll be there tomorrow. Twelve o'clock? Okay. We'll take the bus from Treviso to Vittorio Veneto, and you can pick us up from there."

Debbie looked at me as I was hanging up, and said, "But we already have something planned for tomorrow. Who was that?"

"It was Loredana and Alfieri. They're getting the family together for lunch tomorrow to see us. We have to go." I could see that Debbie wasn't happy about the family changing our plans.

The next morning, we got up early, walked to the Venice train station, took the train to Treviso, and walked to the bus station. It was about ten forty-five, and we got on the bus, waiting for the eleven o'clock departure. The bus to Vittorio Veneto departed once an hour, and this one would get us there right at twelve.

"I'm hungry," Debbie announced.

"That's good", I replied. "Because we're going for lunch, and you know how big lunch is with the relatives."

"But I'm hungry *now*," she insisted, a bit annoyed at my response. "Look, there's a McDonald's right across the street,"

"But honey, it's ten fifty-three. The bus leaves in seven minutes. You'll never make it."

"Yes, I will." She left the bus and headed across the street. Although she could cook some of the best food I had ever tasted, she had a secret love of fast food, especially burgers. Years ago, back in Florida, I used her desire for fast food to hook her into marrying me. Sitting on the bus in Treviso, I was thinking back to that day:

I called her at her office. "Debbie, I'm bringing lunch to your office today, okay?" She agreed, suspecting nothing. I grabbed my picnic basket and headed to McDonald's. After picking up a couple of Big Macs and two orders of fries, I stopped at Burger King for Whoppers, sundae pies, and onion rings. The last stop was at Checkers for a bacon cheeseburger and some chili-cheese fries.

Debbie was surprised to see the picnic basket when I arrived at her office. "Honey, you know I can't go anywhere for a picnic, can't we just eat here?"

"Perfect," I replied. "We'll have a picnic at your desk." She chuckled as I brought out a tablecloth, cloth napkins, and paper plates. A puzzled look appeared on her face as the burgers began to pile up on her plate. I handed her a red rose and stood silently.

She looked at it, and politely said, "Thanks." It was, after all, a bit curious that I would give her a fake red rose, when sitting on her desk was a dozen real yellow roses I had sent the day before. Seeing that I wasn't moving, she examined the rose more carefully to see what was so special about it. She soon noticed the hinge on the rose and opened it.

I dropped to one knee. "Debbie, will you marry me?" The emerald and diamond ring sparkled from inside the fake rose.

She fell back in her chair. "Yes, *yes!*" As for the hamburgers, they sat until dinner, as she was far too excited to eat lunch.

The bus driver got on the bus, jolting me back to the present, to Treviso, and to the fact that Debbie was still not on the bus. I waited, staring at the clock. 10:54, 10:55, 10:56, 10:57, and no Debbie. At 10:58, the driver started the bus.

I thought, "What if she doesn't return before the bus leaves? If I get off the bus now and wait for her, we'll have to take the next bus and arrive at one o'clock, an hour late. What would I tell my family? That we were an hour late for lunch because my wife wanted a McDonald's hamburger before joining them for lunch? Or should I stay on the bus hoping that as it passed McDonald's, she would abandon her position in line and get on the bus?" I took my chances and stayed on the bus. At a minute after eleven, the driver pulled away. He turned in front of the McDonald's and drove slowly past. Debbie didn't come out, and I couldn't see any sign of her. As the bus picked up speed and headed out of town, I realized that I had just left Debbie in Treviso with no return ticket to Venice and not enough money to purchase one. And what would I say to the relatives when I showed up without her?

Loredana waved from her car as I got off the bus in Vittorio Veneto. Looking perplexed, she asked, "Where's Debbie?"

"She ran into a... a clothing store, yep, that's it, a clothing store, and the bus left without her," I lied.

"And you left your wife in a strange city and stayed on the bus?" she asked sternly.

"Well, it isn't really that strange of a city," I offered weakly. She didn't smile.

"So what will Debbie do, stuck in Treviso? Where will she go?"

I thought for a bit. "I suppose she'll take the next bus. But it's not for another hour."

We drove to the house where all the aunts, uncles, nephews, and nieces came out to greet us at the car. "Where's Debbie?" they all asked. Loredana explained about the clothing store.

"And you mean he just left her there all alone?" was the common reply. It occurred to me that as far as the family was concerned, I might as well have left Debbie on a tiny island with sharks circling. Clearly, I had made a bad decision. I couldn't confide that I had actually left her at McDonald's where she went to grab a quick hamburger before heading to their house to eat lunch. No one spoke to me for the next half hour, at which point Loredana and I returned to the bus station. The next bus arrived.

"Debbie, I'm so glad you are safe," I said as she got off the bus.

Clearly furious, she walked right by me and greeted Loredana with a big hug. "I got off the bus for a moment—" she started.

Loredana interrupted, "To go into a clothing store. We heard. I can't believe he left you there. Let's go to the house, and you can have a nice glass of wine and something to eat." I sat in the back silently, as Loredana and Debbie caught up on the local gossip.

After getting the cold shoulder from everyone during dinner, I mentioned to Loredana that the last bus back to Treviso was leaving in thirty minutes. We got back in her car, but not before one of my uncles told me once again that a good husband would never leave his wife in a foreign city all alone.

"Clothing store?" Debbie asked once we were back on the train from Treviso to Venice, "Why the hell did you tell them I was in a clothing store? They wanted to see what I bought."

"You could have showed them the French fries you have in your purse," I said, but only to myself.

The next time we visited relatives, we rented a car. Debbie hid the McDonald's bag in the car before we arrived.

Keep Your Receipt

A wonderful Italian holiday treat, *panettone* looked like a soufflé but was actually more of a bread. Frequently almost a foot high, the cone-shaped holiday breads often contained candied fruit and had a small amount of sugar on top. They were sold in every grocery store around Christmas, but rare was the bakery which still made a quality product. In light of this, I called upon my friend Davide, born in Venice, to guide me to the best *panettone* in town.

"There is a small *panificio* in the Dorsoduro neighborhood that makes absolutely the best Focaccia Veneziane," he said. He armed me with typical Venetian directions. "When you get to the square, go over the bridge and down the calle; it is a little way on the right." During my school break on Monday, I went in search of *panettone*. After wandering around for fifteen minutes, I asked the lady at the corner newspaper store where the *panificio* could be found.

"Just walk about thirty or forty steps down that way, you can't miss it." I walked seventy or eighty steps in the required direction and stopped when I reached the high water, which was pouring over onto the *calle* in the lowest places. With my break over, I returned to school.

Most stores in Venice didn't have signs with their name posted above the store. When the store was closed, the metal shutters were pulled down in front of the windows leaving no visible trace of the delicious items hiding on the other side. A quick check in my book of artisan shops revealed that the *panificio* was closed every Monday and Wednesday. Returning the next morning, Tuesday, I was more certain of the location. Still not finding the elusive treasure of *panettone*, a quick check with a nearby restaurant revealed the exact location. The owner of the restaurant, seeing the hopeless look on my face, walked me directly to the store two doors away. "Closed Monday and Tuesday" was the only sign posted on the shutters.

It was a cool, crisp, and sunny Wednesday morning when I returned to the familiar spot only to find all but one of the shutters closed. One had been raised to a height of about two feet, indicating the possibility that not only might they still be in business, but that they might be busy preparing their delicacies for us unfortunate souls destined to remain on the wrong side of the shutters.

By Thursday, the other students were also curious about this *panificio* and their well-known, but seemingly unobtainable, products. "Let us know what you find," one said. What I found was a bakery open and ready for business but completely devoid of products on the shelves.

"My friend Davide told me that you make the best *panettone* in Venice," I said.

The old woman smiled, and the old man behind her said, "Focaccia, yes. They will be ready this evening. Come back then or tomorrow morning." I ran back to class eager to share the news with the other students. Christmas was coming soon, and I wanted to taste their *panettone* while it was still available.

Friday morning at break, the three of us, Lynn from Holland, Yuko from Japan, and I, made the trek to this Mecca of *panettone*. The shelves were filled with panettone, apple tarts, radicchio tarts, cookies dipped in a smooth dark chocolate, and ricotta pie.

"This is a dream come true!" Yuko said. The couple delighted in giving us pieces of everything to taste. The solid chocolate had a flavor smoother and richer than any I had ever tasted.

"Can I please have another piece for my wife?" I asked.

"Give him two," the old man said. "He will eat one, and his wife will never get to try it!"

We each purchased a sack full of goodies, including the *panettone*, which as it turned out was not *panettone* at all. It was Venetian Focaccia, a bread made with an ancient type of yeast no longer used in most bakeries. The top had a thin layer of glazed sugar, just enough to give it a shiny appearance.

Grabbing our bags and our receipts, we headed into the street. "This chocolate is so good it must be illegal!"

I said. Lynn didn't hear me, as she had walked right into one of three policemen who had been standing outside the door but hidden from view.

"Give me your receipts," the policeman ordered. We each handed over our receipts. As I pulled mine out of my pocket, I noticed that it wasn't a real receipt, but merely an adding machine tape indicating the total purchase amount. The owners of the store had been skimming. By not recording the purchase on the cash register, they could pocket the money without paying taxes. The policeman ordered us back into the store and, in front of the store owners, asked us if we had purchased the items in our bag from this store. We assured him that we had, and he told us to leave.

"But what about my receipt?" I asked.

"You should go now."

The couple behind the counter appeared terrorized with fear over what would happen next. Lynn cried as she described our experience to the rest of the class.

"The fines for tax skimming are enormous," our professor explained. "Some stores have been forced to close after the *Guardia di Finanza* police squads have shown up." Later, Davide explained that the fine was fifteen hundred euro per incident. With the three of us, their fine would have been forty-five hundred euro.

Davide also explained that the cash register receipt was like a legal contract between the buyer and seller. A customer leaving the store without a receipt was subject to a fine of five hundred euro. "You are required to keep your receipt until you have traveled one kilometer from the store," he said.

Gulp! I thought back to all those times I had bought a coffee or ice cream cone and left the receipt on the counter.

At *Pasticceria Il Bucintoro*, Gino confirmed this law. "Once, I was fined just for giving a piece of candy in a bag to a child. The police were waiting outside."

At home, I tried to enjoy the incredible pastries from the *panificio*, but my imagined image of the family being subjected to such steep fines took the sweetness out of the focaccia and soured the flavor of the chocolate. "We learned more about Venice during break then we did in class," I remembered Yuko saying as school let out.

It was months before I had the courage to return to the little family bakery. While I felt bad, almost as if it had somehow been our fault, the thought of their tasty treats brought me back. I once again loaded up on goodies, gave them my money, and placed the adding machine tape I received as a receipt in my pocket and headed out the door.

No Class

Attending Istituto Venezia five days a week had been enlightening. Since October, we had been learning Italian with other students from around the world, with Italian as our only common language. But it was the last day of class for some of us. After three months, we had finished level five, the final level, and it was time to celebrate. Mia, a student from Sweden also graduating that day, and I secretly entered the school secretary's office at 12:55, took the bell, and hid in the hallway. At precisely one o'clock, Mia and I, each with one hand on the bell, ran down the hallway ringing it as hard and as loud as we could. We continued running up and down the hall ringing the bell until one of the professors took it away from us.

School was over for some of us, and Christmas break was here, so it was a bittersweet day as we celebrated with the other students sharing Prosecco at Imagina, the local café. Debbie still had two months to go, as she had just completed level three. She celebrated with a *caffe corretto con grappa*. Mia would be returning to Sweden and Yuko to Japan, but Debbie and I would be staying here, in our new home in Venice.

Christmas in Venice

An occasional snowfall covered the boats, bridges, and *calli*, making walking difficult and often dangerous.

There were no guardrails to stop someone from sliding off the walkway and into the canals. The tourists were gone, and a sense of peace and family enveloped the lagoon.

"Over-commercialization of Christmas" had become the phrase we used to describe the celebration of the holiday in the United States. Long before Halloween, we would start to hear familiar carols in the malls throughout the fifty states. Thus, our first Christmas in Italy was a bit of a culture shock. Thanksgiving had come and gone, and there was still no sign that Santa was coming. No lights hanging in the windows, no trees, no songs in the stores, no store shelves full of decorations. We couldn't even find Christmas cards. Debbie and I could scarcely believe it. Where was Christmas?

In Venice, Christmas was simply a religious holiday. Parishioners went to church quietly with their families, as they did every Sunday, and prayed. A typical Venetian Christmas dinner consisted of scallops *alla Veneziana*, risotto *di pesce*, *Baccala*—salted cod—*alla Vicentina*, and polenta. After a light dessert of *panettone*, they retired, feeling a sense of renewal from the meaning of the day. It was a time when Venetians slowed even more than normal.

After the twelfth of December, small signs began to give an indication that Christmas was not forgotten. On a canal just off of Strada Nova in Cannaregio, there was a

Christmas tree boat. There, we could buy a tree, along with a bucket and some dirt. Of course, we couldn't just strap it to the top of a car and drive home. How were we going to get the tree back to our apartment on the other side of the Grand Canal? Debbie and I stopped at a café to devise a plan. Fortified by our 'corrected' coffee drinks, we went to the Christmas tree boat.

We picked out a tree, carried it to the Grand Canal, and boarded a *traghetto*, one of the gondolas used solely for crossing the Grand Canal. We rode the gondola standing, holding our tree, and then walked the remaining quarter mile to the house with each of us holding one end of the tree. I repeated the trip, crossing the Grand Canal two more times, once with the bucket and then with the fifty-pound bag of dirt. We found a small string of lights in an electric store and a few ornaments in the COIN department store. After surrounding the tree with three or four poinsettias, we were set for the holiday.

The process took the entire day and a good portion of the night. We collapsed into bed, thankful Christmas only came once a year.

On Christmas Eve, we attended mass at the Frari and listened to the glorious sounds of the pipe organ and the choir filling that seven-hundred-year-old church. Walking back to the apartment late at night, we could hear carols emanating from the various churches. The boats were all docked, the water still, and the sounds of *Volare* were non-existent. A light fog covered the city. It was truly a silent, holy night.

The Grim Reaper Visits

New Year's Eve was swiftly approaching. Our daughter Stephanie returned to Italy to celebrate the coming New Year with us, an experience to which we all looked forward with excitement. *Piazza San Marco* was filled with thousands of revelers drinking and watching live concerts in Venice's largest square, while fireworks erupted in the lagoon.

Unfortunately, the New Year's Eve celebration had been cancelled out of respect for the victims of the Indian Ocean Tsunami just days before. Despite this, Venetians seemed to migrate to *Piazza San Marco*, propelled by tradition. Arriving at the square, we found thousands of people drinking to excess with no organized activities. Empty bottles of *Bellini*, the Venetian drink of Prosecco and peach juice, littered the piazza. Feeling that nothing good could come from the crowd, we went to a friend's house on the other side of town.

Francesco and his girlfriend Mirela welcomed us for dinner. After a delightful meal comprised mainly of some "Creatures from the Venetian Lagoon," we relaxed with wine and a variety of *grappa*.

Singing the entire one-hour walk home, we took care not to fall into the cold water of the many canals in our path.

Upon entering our apartment, Freckles greeted us with tail wagging, while Alexandria slept on the couch. Moments later, Stephanie screamed. "Alexandria! She's not moving!"

Debbie's cat and companion of over ten years had died. She was curled up peacefully on the couch, but was certainly no longer with the living. Debbie broke down in a corner of the room and wailed. We comforted her, but then the reality of the situation hit me. What was I to do with Alexandria? Debbie, through her tears, made me promise to give her a good burial, complete with the blanket she had loved. So, I wrapped her cat in the blanket, put her in a box, wrapped the box tightly with duct tape, made a handle, and placed the box outside for the night.

The next morning, after promising Debbie once more that I would take good care of Alexandria, I left with the box. But what to do? It wasn't as if we had a back yard I could dig up to bury the cat. We were living on an island built upon millions and millions of tree trunks pounded into the muck and topped with stone.

From the train station, I phoned my Venetian friends. "We just give the animal back to the veterinarian and aren't really sure what they do with it," one responded. Another informed me that in Italy it was illegal to bury a pet, due to health concerns. Finally, my uncle who lived an hour north of Venice in the country, told me that while I couldn't bury the cat on his property, one of the neighbors would allow me to bury it in his vineyard.

So, armed with a cat in a box, I took the next train to Conegliano, where my uncle picked me up at the train station. For the twenty-minute drive to his home in Sarmede, he just kept looking from me to the box and laughing. While the cat waited patiently outside in the box, my aunt made lunch. We ate and caught up on events.

After lunch, Alfieri showed me the new home they had built just a few feet away for their eighteen-year-old son, Giovanni. In this part of Italy, there was a tradition of building a home nearby for your firstborn son. The boy wasn't allowed to move into the house until he was married, usually in his mid-thirties. This provided a certain incentive for him to live near his parents, and thus to care for them in their old age. Currently, Alfieri's mother Agosta lived downstairs, with Loredana and Alfieri living upstairs.

On occasion, the housing plans ran awry. Another cousin of mine who lived nearby had everything ready for him. His parents had purchased a five-bedroom house with two kitchens and marble throughout the inside, only a few blocks away from them. All he had to do was get married. Of course, he would have had to marry a girl who met with his parents' approval. He found a girl, of whom his parents didn't approve, and so the pair eloped to a nearby town and rented an apartment. Having no other sons, the parents promptly sold the house, gaining a tidy sum for their retirement.

From across the street, Francesco, the neighbor, greeted us. A tall man with dark hair and a small moustache, he was retired from the Italian railroads. He hunted, grew grapes for Prosecco and Malvasia, caught birds and rabbits, tended his vegetable garden, and tinkered in his workshop. Visible in the workshop was a motorcycle in the midst of being rebuilt and a polenta maker crafted from a washing machine motor and screen mesh. In the loft was an old table, which Francesco had years ago told me that my mother used when she was a child to help make silk. He had explained something about the silkworms living in the box on one end, and the rest I didn't understand, as my knowledge of the Italian language didn't include the lives of silkworms.

As we crossed the street, I saw that he was making a broom from corn stalks.

"I have all my hunting dogs buried here," Francesco said, pointing to the edge of his vineyard. "Each of them is buried next to one of these poles at the end of the row. I have one spot left, and you can use that one for your cat." He dug a hole, and I opened the box, placed the cat and the blanket in the hole, and stopped. A crowd had gathered. My aunt, uncle, Francesco, his wife, and another neighbor all stood looking at me.

"Well, aren't you going to say something?" my aunt asked.

I hadn't prepared a eulogy for the cat, much less one in Italian. So, my impromptu eulogy went something like this: "Here lies Alexandria. She was a cat, but not too fat. She was alive, and now she is not. So today we say goodbye."

My aunt stared blankly at me. I could see a smirk on my uncle's face. "To the wine cellar," he said.

6

THE GRASS IS GREENER ON THE OTHER SIDE OF THE CANAL

The New Apartment

Sitting outside in our garden in the early evening—it was too dark to sit out there later at night, now that the electricians had disconnected our garden light—I reflected on life in a ground-floor apartment in Venice. The humidity was tremendous. We had purchased three dehumidifiers that used small tablets to draw water out of the air and into little buckets, which had to be emptied daily. But still, the clothes we had set out on a folding clothesline inside the apartment wouldn't dry, even after four days. We had given up on leaving the clothes outside to dry, as it seemed to rain every other day in the winter, making that option impossible.

My wife walked out holding a sack full of shoes, Prada, Ferragamo, and Louboutin, among others. "Look at these shoes. They're all ruined," she said, laying the sack at my feet. A light green mold covered the shoes, much as it tended to grow on the walls in the ground floor apartments. The humidity seeped through the floor providing a perfect environment for it to grow, especially in the wintertime when the windows remained shut. Once a week, we wiped the walls with a water and bleach solution to remove the mold before it attached itself. But never did we think that it would take over the shoes in the closets. "

Living on the ground floor is not healthy," our friends had said. "The humidity seeps into your bones, and your back will ache." After five months in Venice, we had come to understand these problems of *piano terra*, or ground-floor living. The humidity, lack of light, lack of a real oven, and lack of legal rental contract led us to the decision to find a different apartment for the remainder of our year in Venice.

"Thank God," our landlord said, when informed of our desire to move. "Ever since you came here, the entire building has been full of the smells of your wife's roasts, pies, and sauces."

The apartment rental agency lady, Raffaella, or possibly Betta, her twin, understood our decision to leave. "I'll help you find a better apartment. We will find a well-lit apartment with an oven and away from the ground floor." I reminded Raffaella that we also needed a legal rental contract. The search was on.

I mentioned to Rosetta, Renzo, and Luca at the local café that we were looking for a new apartment. Immediately, a stranger standing next to me at the bar scribbled a name on a piece of paper. "The Buzato brothers. They own many apartments in Venice, and they live right down the *calle*. Head toward the pizzeria, and you will see their name on the door right after the place where the big brown dog lives."

I took her note and saved it in my pocket. Rosetta mentioned that she would get the word out, and she did.

"I hear you are looking for an apartment," Viviana at the local electricity store said later that afternoon. "That's a shame because I just rented one for the next six months."

When I returned to the café that evening, Rosetta handed me the name of someone else with an available apartment, but offered this caution, "I don't know anything about the apartment, but the owner is very nice."

The rental agency called the next day. "You must come look at this apartment in Cannaregio today. It is on the sixth floor with an elevator, and there is plenty of light. And the contract is a legal contract." Raffaella's voice sounded urgent. We agreed to meet that afternoon.

At first glance, Cannaregio appeared to be a very touristy part of Venice. Strada Nova, the walkway winding its way from the train station toward the Rialto Bridge, was full of suitcase-toting visitors feeling either lost or amazed by their surroundings. A few meters off this well-beaten path, however, was a Venice that most tourists never saw— calm canals with residents going about their normal daily routine.

Our prior neighborhood, Santa Croce, had no street markets or fish vendors. Other than one square, Campo San Giacomo dell'Orio, it had very little life at all. Cannaregio, on the other hand, had vendors selling fruits, vegetables, fish, and clothing right outside our door. Cannaregio, the birthplace of Casanova, Venice's most famous lover, had life. While it certainly had its share of tourists, the cafés were full of locals discussing politics, and the side *calli* were full of bakeries, fresh pasta vendors, and vibrant restaurants. Cannaregio was the living part of Venice. *That* was where we wanted to be.

We met at a nearby café. Debbie and Raffaella each had a *caffe corretto con grappa* while I stuck with my normal macchiato. We walked down Rio Cannaregio and into the Ghetto.

The Ghetto is the place in Venice where the Jews were allowed to live in the 16th century. Like the Jews, many groups of people had their own islands, including the Germans and the Dalmations. Venice, built by a population seeking refuge, became a safe haven for outcasts of many types from around the world. Even lepers and lunatics had their own islands. This one, however, was the Ghetto, named because before the Jews arrived, an iron foundry was located there. In Venetian slang, the word "*geto*" was used to describe either the foundry itself, or some of the products made there. Some speculated that the word "geto" meant "thrown away," or "jettisoned," as it was the area where the scraps from the foundry were discarded. It had been pronounced "jet-o," but the first Jews to arrive were of Germanic descent and pronounced the word with a hard G, hence the term *Ghetto* today. "Wait till I call my father and tell him we are moving into the ghetto!" I thought.

The apartment was beautiful. From the other end of the island, I could see the bell tower in Piazza San Marco from our window. We had three bedrooms, a living room, dining room, bathroom, washing machine, and an oven! No, wait. No oven. "Doesn't anyone in this town have an oven?" my wife exclaimed, exasperated. "We do most of our cooking on the stove," the landlord, Mariella, offered. "But we will get you a countertop oven."

And we had an elevator. In Venice. In the town where only the fanciest of hotels have an elevator, here we were on the sixth floor with an elevator. We were in heaven. The apartment was high enough off of the ground that we wouldn't have problems with mold, and we were in a residential district with great markets, quick access to the train station, and great views. We signed the papers and began packing.

Moving Day – Again

We had the weekend to move. By Sunday night, we had to be out of our ground-floor location and have all of the things we had accumulated moved into the new apartment.

The plan was perfect. There was a *vaporetto* boat station just a quarter of a mile from our current apartment, and the *vaporetto* stopped immediately in front of the new one. I could take the suitcases, computers, tables, dog crate, appliances, and guitar, everything a little at a time to the *vaporetto*, across the Grand Canal, up the elevator, and into the new apartment. We would start Saturday morning.

I arrived at the *vaporetto* station to see a tremendous commotion in the water. Protesters were everywhere, and the merchant boats had blocked the Grand Canal. It seemed that the police chief had decided to enforce the speed limit in the canals, and the merchant ships had protested by blocking the waterway. There would be no *vaporetti* that day.

Heavy with baggage, I walked over seven bridges, including the Ponte Degli Scalzi, one of only three crossing the Grand Canal. It was over two miles to our new apartment. Exhausted, I dropped off my first load, and made the two-mile trek back to the old apartment. While preparing a second load, I explained the situation to Debbie. "Wait until tomorrow," she said. After making one more four-mile, fourteen-bridge round trip, I surrendered for the day. The next day, the protesters would be gone, and I could carry the bulk of the items by boat. In fact, on TV that night, the newscasters explained that the police chief had changed his mind and decided not to enforce the speed limit. The merchants had won.

The next morning, I arrived at the *vaporetto* station only to see another commotion in the Grand Canal. Gondolas were everywhere, blocking the canal. The gondoliers were protesting the police chief's decision to ignore the speed limit, and they would be keeping the Grand Canal closed for the entire day. I heard later that one gondolier had even carried his gondola to the top of the Rialto bridge, blocking it to pedestrians, causing one seventy-year-old Venetian to jump in the Grand Canal and swim across. He was brought to the hospital for observation, due to the pollution in the water. Clearly, there would again be no *vaporetti*. I made the four-mile round trip six times that day, each time with suitcases weighing fifty pounds or more. Over fourteen hours from when I started, the move had been completed. The next morning I looked out my window at the beautiful view. I could see traffic moving normally on the Grand Canal, and the *vaporetto* pulling up to the dock six floors below.

Gastone

"Excuse me, have you seen my cat?" asked the proud elderly man standing in the hallway outside our door. I had seen him before, entering his apartment two floors below, on the fourth floor. He never seemed to venture any farther than the corner before returning home. Tonight he seemed troubled. "It's a small rust-colored cat. I call her Rosa. She got out the window sometime today and didn't come back. Ever since my wife died..." He stopped for a minute, wiped his eyes, and regained his composure. "No matter. But if you see her, please bring her to my apartment."

"*Si, certo,*" I replied.

Clearly embarrassed at breaking down in public, he shuffled down the stairs back to his apartment. I listened as he inserted the key into the lock, opened, and then slowly shut his door. The sounds echoed through the quiet staircase.

Standing outside our door, I explained to Debbie, who had come out to see what was going on, about the old man and his missing cat. We knew what we had to do and left the apartment immediately in search of his pet. We were familiar with most of the outside cats in our neighborhood, so Rosa wouldn't be very difficult to spot. We searched all seven floors, then walked around the outside of the building with no luck. I even walked down to the spot near Ponte delle Guglie where the *pescatore* sold his fish every morning, since the cats seemed to gather there in search of scraps. Back in the days of the plagues, cats were brought to Venice to reduce the number of rats and mice that caused the spread of the plague. But since the 1990s, most of the twelve thousand feral cats had been sterilized or exiled to other islands, a fact for which the booming rat and mouse population was thankful.

Walking up the stairway back at the apartment, we heard a cat crying. Sitting outside our door was a rust-colored cat. "Is this Rosa?" I asked the old man when he opened his apartment door.

"Rosa, Rosa, where did you go?" he asked, taking her from my arms. Obviously relieved, he turned back to me and said, "Please come in for a cup of coffee."

It was in this way that I met Gastone.

The Pharmacy

Gastone was a very private man, and his story revealed itself slowly over our remaining months in Venice. Born in Egypt, he spent his life in Venice. His daughter Mariella was our landlord, and his son Massimiliano, or Maxi, lived above us on the seventh floor. Maxi explained that since Gastone's wife died about a year earlier, Gastone had become a recluse. Once or twice a week, he would go to the local café to have a coffee, but then he would return directly home. On Sundays, he would take the *vaporetto* to Lido and walk to the cemetery to spend time at his wife's gravesite in the Jewish cemetery.

I asked Gastone if I could stop in for a coffee now and then. Debbie invited him for dinner. Eventually, Gastone and I fell into a routine. Six days a week I would knock on his door at eight thirty in the morning, wait for him to dress in his suit, and walk him to the *Torrefazione* Marchi Caffé Costarica for coffee. Since 1930, the *Torrefazione* has had saucers and spoons lining the counter, always ready for customers to order either an espresso or a macchiato. We each had a punch card for coffee and took turns paying the check. Gastone would lean over the counter while I sat back on the fifty-pound bags of coffee beans piled three feet high, the aroma of roasting coffee beans filling the room. We walked arm in arm to the fruit and vegetable market, the fish market—he loved sardines— and the bakery. Occasionally, he would ask me if it was okay if we stopped at his doctor's office near San Marcuola to pick up a prescription. His doctor's office had two rooms, one where the doctor administered to patients, and the other a waiting room with two couches and a coffee table. There was no receptionist and no long hallways with scores of patients, just those two rooms. On top of the coffee table was a shoebox full of envelopes. Gastone flipped through them until he found the one with his name, opened the envelope, removed the prescription, and returned the well-worn envelope to its place in the box. With the prescription in his suit pocket, we walked arm in arm to the *farmacia* to fill the prescription.

In Italy, each time a prescription was filled, the paper was stamped and returned to the customer with the medication. Once the number of stamps on the paper reached the maximum number of refills prescribed, it could no longer be stamped.

Each week we returned to the pharmacy, but this time the pharmacist shook her head, and said, "I'm sorry, but I cannot stamp your old prescription because it has already been filled three times. Can you see here where the doctor has written the number three?" Gastone agreed, whereupon she said, "That will be five euro for the medication." We left with the medication, but without a fourth stamp on the paper. In twisted Italian logic, the number of refills on the prescription was loosely interpreted as the number of times that the pharmacist could stamp the prescription indicating that it had been refilled. Dispensing the medication, however, didn't seem to be a problem.

"It's an important law, this one about refills; it's just not very practical," Gastone explained, as he placed both the medication and his prescription into his suit pocket, certain to use it again the following month.

The Boys

Following the instructions Gastone had given me the day before, I didn't visit him at eight thirty as usual, but instead picked him up at precisely twenty minutes after ten. "*I ragazzi*, the boys, want to meet you," he had said, without offering any explanation. "We will meet them at Ponte delle Guglie at ten thirty, so pick me up at ten twenty." The bridges seemed to be common meeting spots, and Ponte delle Guglie was only two hundred yards from our apartment building.

"*Ciao, bello.* You are sure dressed nice today," Gastone said as I arrived. I wore a button-down shirt, dress pants, and my best shoes, to make a good impression on "*I Ragazzi,*" whoever they were.

Standing at the bridge were three men, all apparently in their eighties, looking at their watches. "*Ciao,* Gastone. Is this him?" asked the tallest, pointing in my direction.

"*Si*, his name is Barry Frangipane," offered Gastone.

"Barry? Is that a name?" inquired the tall one. He appeared to be the leader of the group.

"It's an American name. They don't always use names from the Bible," Gastone explained.

"Hmm, curious. We'll just call him Frangipane," the leader said. "*Piacere*, Frangipane. *Sono* Franco. Nice to meet you."

I met Franco, Renzo, and Amedeo. Over time, my daily ritual changed to include a meeting with the boys at ten thirty sharp.

My days started at eight thirty, when I joined Gastone for coffee and went shopping. After unloading his groceries at his apartment, I would turn to leave.

"Sit down, have a cup of coffee," he would say, not wanting the time to end. Over time, Gastone told me stories of him and his wife, life in Venice years ago, and tales of his parents. But at ten twenty-five each day, I would leave his apartment and run down to the Ponte delle Guglie where "the boys" and I would meet before heading to the *Torrefazione* for coffee.

Franco, Renzo, and Amedeo had their own ritual. After coffee, we walked to a different fruit and vegetable stand than the one I had been to earlier with Gastone, a different bakery, and frequently to the butcher. One by one, they would return to their apartments until it was just Amedeo and I walking together to his apartment directly facing Ponte degli Scalzi near the Santa Lucia train station. On a good day, Amedeo would belt out a piece from his favorite opera; on other days, he would point out places of interest, such as the spots where his friends lost their lives during World War II.

"We were part of the resistance," he would say proudly. It was from Amedeo that I would learn which *calli* were once canals, but had been filled in, making it possible for pedestrians to walk. *Rio Tera*, he explained, in dialect meant "filled-in ditch." So, *Rio Tera San Leonardo* would have once been a canal named *San Leonardo*, now filled in to become a walkway.

By noon, I would return to our apartment where Debbie was usually waiting with a fresh lunch prepared from the best market offerings of the morning. After a brief nap, at two o'clock (8:00 AM Eastern Time), I turned on my computer and worked for my U.S. clients until ten fifty-five each evening, while Debbie relaxed watching DVDs from the movie rental machine just off of Strada Nova. When finished working, I closed my laptop, walked down to the gelateria before the eleven o'clock closing for a cone of pistachio gelato, returned Debbie's movies, then strolled along the quiet canals enjoying the solitude and the reflection of the moon on the water.

Most of my clients never knew that I had moved to Italy. My internet telephone with a Florida number worked just fine in Venice, and since I was always available during standard New York business hours, no one suspected a thing. On occasion, a client would say, "I see there is a hurricane in the Gulf. Are you feeling the effects yet?" After a quick check of the storm's location and after reviewing the current weather in Tampa, I would issue the proper response.

The Hospital

Debbie was doubled over in pain. "What is it?" I asked.

"My stomach—it hurts really bad," she replied. After waiting for a few hours, it was clear that it was something serious that was not going to go away. It was Saturday afternoon, and none of the doctors' offices were open. Our landlord recommended taking Debbie to the emergency room.

The ambulances were boats, and the emergency entrance was a covered dock. Since the ambulance and the scheduled *vaporetto* both took the same path, we decided just to take the *vaporetto* to the hospital. Mariella went with us to be sure we had no problems.

Debbie and I instinctively got at the end of the line to board. "Come up here, there's space at the front of the dock." Mariella motioned to us.

We were confused. "But the line—" I started.

Mariella interrupted, "Curious, you Americans and your idea of a queue. You are so proper. We do not have queues here in Italy. If there is a space at the front of the dock, we fill it. Why would you wait at the end? The boat could fill up and leave you behind!"

"Why, indeed?" I thought, adjusting to this Italian custom while walking Debbie to the front of the dock.

At the hospital, Debbie was checked in quickly, without all of the paperwork which we were accustomed to in the States. She was seen by two doctors and had an ultrasound, x-rays, and a blood test. The doctors determined that there was nothing serious, and by then whatever had been bothering Debbie had passed, so we decided to return home.

I approached the cashier at the hospital, and he handed me the paperwork, her x-ray, and the ultrasound film. "That will be sixty euro." I handed him my credit card. "I can't take money from you," he said. "We send you a bill. Then you pay."

"But my address is in the United States," I argued. "Can't I just pay now?"

"No, you cannot. If your address is in the United States, maybe you will never get the bill. *Arrivederci.*"

Standing on the *vaporetto* on the way back to the apartment, I remarked, "I can't believe they give the patient all of their medical records and films to keep!"

"Why wouldn't they?" Mariella replied. "You paid for them."

The Electricians – Part Two

The new apartment had only one phone jack, and it was right at the base of the front door. As I had converted the bedroom at the end of the hall into my office, I needed to have phone service in that room, especially since my internet service would be through the same lines, using DSL.

After the fiasco with the electricians in the last apartment, I decided to go with someone I knew this time, someone I trusted. Viviana from the electricity store had helped me in the past, and her husband Paolo was an electrician. When I entered the store, Viviana was sitting in a chair, reading a book to a small girl on her lap. "One of my customers had some errands to run, so I'm watching her daughter," she explained. When I described the work to be done in the new apartment, Viviana went in the back to check with Paolo about helping out. "Paolo would be happy to install the phone line," she said. Sure enough, Paolo showed up the next day at our apartment. He connected fifty feet of phone wire to the outlet at the front door, ran the wire on the floor twenty feet down the hall, drilled a three-inch, round hole in the wall for this tiny wire, and ran the wire into my office. He then threw the wire over the top of the doorjamb and placed a permanent jack on the wall inside my office. I shut my office door, and the phone wire came down from the doorjamb and rested on the floor. Paolo placed the cable back over the doorjamb, and said, "*Non ti preoccupare*. Do not worry. This is only temporary."

He continued, "I'll come back with some molding strips and permanently attach the phone wire to the walls so you don't have this unsightly cable lying on your floor."

Two months later, Viviana and Paolo invited us to their home for dinner. I looked carefully to see if their home had cables running on the floor. No, everything in their house looked neat and tidy. The subject of my apartment never came up, and I thought better than to ask about it. We stayed in the apartment for seven months. Paolo never returned to finish the job. We placed throw rugs on the floor and used thumbtacks to keep the phone wire above the door.

A Great Day for Activation

With the new apartment came the need for a new internet connection. I called Telecom Italia and requested their best internet connection. "You will have your equipment in about ten days," promised the lady at Telecom Italia, the public telephone company. "Once you receive your equipment, your line will be activated a few days later."

For the next ten days, I worked from an internet café. Then a call to Telecom Italia brought assurance that the equipment would be arriving "any day." Any day except today, as it turned out. One month from the time I placed my order, the equipment arrived. At that point, working from the internet café was costing me substantially more than my rent.

A week later, I called my friend at Telecom Italia again. "When will my line be activated?" It was my lucky day. "Tomorrow," came the response. Three times a week for the next two weeks, I called and was assured that my line would be activated "tomorrow."

Finally, I asked my Telecom Italia friend why every time I called she would tell me that my line would be activated tomorrow. On what information was she basing that decision?

"Our computers don't tell us when your line will be activated," she explained. "But tomorrow would *always* be a great day for activation."

Working through the cousin of a friend of a friend, I discovered that Telecom Italia was over their capacity, and that new customers were being activated only as old ones died or quit. This friend suggested that I use a new private company called FastWeb. FastWeb had me connected the following Friday. It was a great day for activation.

7

FRIENDS, NEW AND OLD

While walking in the area of Cà Foscari, the University of Venice, Debbie and I came upon the Venice fire station. The *caserma*, or barracks, had an unassuming front identifiable only by a small sign on the exterior. On the canal, four tunnels provided a method of exit and entry for the fireboats.

We stepped into the foyer and found ourselves surrounded by awards the firemen had won in firefighting competitions as well as a memorial to the firemen lost in fires over the years.

"Can I help you?" Stefano, a tall, blond-haired, blue-eyed fireman in his thirties, introduced himself.

"We're from Florida and have always been curious how a fire station works in this city of water. Would you mind if we looked around?" I asked, sounding a bit more amazed than I really was, hoping to get a tour.

"Stay here, I'll ask the captain," he said, occasionally taking his eyes off of my wife's low-cut blouse and short skirt.

When he returned, Stefano took us for a walk around the fire station. In many ways, it resembled any other fire station, except in the garage there were fire *boats* instead of fire trucks. One of the boats was in obviously better shape than the others, finely varnished and devoid of rust and corrosion. "That's the captain's fireboat," Stefano said proudly. "It can outrun all of the others."

After putting me in a fire suit and a fireman's hat, Stefano explained the process of fighting a fire in Venice. "Our boats just pump the water from the canal straight into the hose. It's very efficient, as long as the hoses are long enough to reach the fire."

"How many fire stations does Venice have?" I asked.

"Just this one," Stefano explained. "It services Venice as well as the islands of Murano, Burano, and Torcello."

Noting the distance between the islands, I asked, "But Burano is quite a distance away. How does that work?"

Stefano sighed. "Not too well. It takes a good twenty minutes to get to Burano. The fire is usually out of control by the time we arrive."

Just then, a bell went off. I anticipated a flurry of activity, with firemen running down the stairs and heading for the boats. But instead, Stefano ushered us out of the garage, and said, "It's dinnertime. Would you care to join us?"

Entering the mess hall, I felt as if I had faded into the background as each fireman carefully inspected Debbie. All were insistent upon having their picture taken individually with her. I glanced around for some cold water, certain that before too long I would need to be putting out *their* fires.

We ate together, with everyone interested in learning more about Debbie. Upon leaving, a young, dark-haired fireman barely out of his twenties leaned over and whispered something to her. "What did he say?" I asked as we walked away.

"Come back sometime without your husband." She chuckled.

Over the following months, Debbie prepared many dishes for our new friends the firemen—lasagna, manicotti, and tiramisu, among others. She enjoyed their cheerful thanks each time we delivered her delectable gifts, but never once did she visit the fire station alone.

Waterfront Dining

As the night set in, when many tourists left and most boats were docked for the night, a peaceful dinner on the banks of a canal in a quiet part of town was a heavenly experience. Nothing could compare with sitting outside in a pigeon-free zone, our table next to the canal, and the water lapping at the seawall by our feet. The moon was rising, and the quiet was only momentarily altered by the passing gondola playing the mandatory *Volare*, or the young Venetian cruising by with rap music blaring out of his boat speakers.

As you converse with your dinner companion while admiring the scenery, the flower salesmen will only stop by a few times to offer you a rose you could purchase for your date. As the salesman hands the flower to her, the *"fiorista"* will watch to see whether you come up with some slick way of asking your date to return the flower, or if instead, you will simply pay his highly inflated price for a flower in need of mouth-to-petal resuscitation.

It was on such a night that I sat outside a small restaurant in Cannaregio with Debbie and our friend Dona from Florida. Dona had been with us for over a week, reviewing the marvels of this city built on water.

"What a marvelous vacation this has been," she said. "You two certainly know your way around this city. Because of you, I have truly experienced Venice. And this dinner is the perfect way to end it."

Admittedly, it was a bit difficult to hear her comments over the sound of the approaching fireboat. As the boat raced to the fire, Stefano waved from the deck. Just then, the wake from the boat swamped our table and soaked us from the waist down. "Now, Dona, you have truly experienced Venice." I laughed, handing her a cloth napkin with which to dry herself.

Yeast

Debbie decided to make a pizza. "Barry, please run to the store and get me some yeast."

"Sure, dear, no problem." After running down six flights of stairs, through the ghetto, and down the *calle* to our neighborhood store, I discovered that they had no yeast. Visiting two other stores produced the same result. Throngs of tourists seemed permanently positioned in such a way to prevent residents from performing their daily duties.

I tended to equate Venice to the Magic Kingdom in Florida. All the tourists walked down Main Street, USA, or Strada Nova and Rio Terá San Leonardo in Venice, heading toward Cinderella's castle, or St. Mark's Square. After a bit of time in those touristy squares, eating at fake restaurants that served only the food which tourists expected, they returned to the train station, or cruise ship, and went home, thinking they had seen Venice. In the meanwhile, however, they jammed up the *calli* making it nearly impossible to rush out and buy something as simple as yeast.

Finally, up four flights of stairs, I asked our friend Claudio where I could find yeast. "At the bakery," he said. "Where else?"

Where else, indeed. Walking into a tiny bakery across town, Il Mondo Del Pane, The World of Bread, I was greeted with a cheery *"Ciao! Buona sera!"* from the owner, in her Murano accent.

"*Ciao*. Debbie sent me out for yeast. Do you have any?"

"What are you making?"

"Pizza."

"For how many?"

"For two people."

She took out a sheet of paper, poured roughly one tablespoon of yeast on the paper, folded it up, and handed it to me. "That will be five cents." As I left, she closed her store for the evening, undoubtedly looking forward to her boat ride home to Murano.

"Debbie, I got the yeast!" I exclaimed triumphantly, like a hunter returning to the cave with the day's catch.

"Great!" she said, not looking at the small envelope. "Paola and Giovanni called, and they will be joining us with their children, so there will be seven of us for dinner. So, I'll make three pizzas. Where's the yeast?"

Looking at our rationed supply of yeast, we opted for pasta instead.

Herbal Suicide

Our new apartment had plenty of sun, and the window ledge seemed like a great place to plant a bit of basil, just as I had seen in other apartments around Venice, many of which had built-in flowerboxes. We would have to settle for planting herbs in freestanding flower pots. While Debbie was at the Rialto fish market, I ran out to purchase the basil, dirt, and container. I had just finished getting everything on the windowsill when she returned.

"Look, honey, I got you some herbs and planted them right here on the windowsill. Now you can have fresh basil without running down to the market!" I said excitedly.

"That was sweet of you, but are you sure the pot will be safe out there?".

"Safe? We're on the sixth floor. I can't imagine anyone stealing it up here," I replied.

About a week later, Debbie came into my office while I was working. "Barry, have you seen the basil? It's not on the windowsill." I rushed to the window, and sure enough, it was gone. But six floors down, in the neighbor's courtyard, was a smashed flowerpot and a small green plant splattered on the ground. I was stunned.

"Wow, honey. I never knew the suicide rate among basil plants was so high." Debbie was not amused, as the market was already closed for the day, and she would have to make her sauce without basil. I purchased a replacement plant the next morning, with a sturdier and more stable base. The second basil plant didn't commit suicide until almost two weeks later.

Back in 1310, a popular uprising occurred in Venice. As the crowd entered Piazza San Marco, an old lady was said to have dropped a flowerpot from her window, killing the flag bearer and causing the leader, Tiepolo, and his followers to run for safety, thus ending the revolt. I now wonder if this historic event was actually the result of her basil pot having jumped from the window onto the troops marching down below, and the old lady had merely looked out of her window to find that her plant, which had just committed herbal suicide, had saved the Venetian republic.

Everything is Relative

With the arrival of spring came better weather and phone calls from Italian relatives. "*Ciao*, Barry. It's Franco Frangipane in Sicily. Rosa Maria and I would like to come to Venice next week and see you and Debbie. Can we stay at your apartment?"

Franco was my uncle from the hometown of the Frangipane family in Ciminna, just outside of Palermo. As the music director of his local high school, he had only been in Venice for brief trips with the student band. Franco and his wife wanted to see Venice through the eyes of the locals, that was, through our eyes.

At dinner that night, Debbie and I planned the itinerary. We would show Franco and Rosa Maria the secret gardens of Venice and the serene canals near Fondamenta Misericordia along the backside of Cannaregio. We would share the Rialto market at sunrise and Piazza San Marco at midnight.

During their visit, Debbie prepared local dishes including *Vitello Tonnato*, a thinly sliced veal roast in a tuna sauce, and Risotto *alla Parmigiana*, a risotto with Parmesan cheese.

"How did you learn to cook these northern Italian specialties so well?" Rosa Maria asked. Debbie just smiled and served the Tiramisu.

Spring also brought my cousin Irma and her husband Massimo from Milan, along with their two children. Even Alfieri and Loredana stayed with us overnight. "You two know this town better than we do, and we have lived an hour away for our entire lives," Loredana commented.

While enjoying the sun at a café in Campo Santo Stefano, Venice's second largest square, I pointed to one of the bell towers nearby, and asked, "Alfieri, so many of these towers are leaning. Doesn't Italy have any good architects?"

Alfieri, ever the proud Italian, folded his arms, took off his sunglasses, and looked me in the eye. "These towers were built hundreds of years before your country was even a dream. If they want to lean a little, let them. They have earned the right. And besides, compared to the tower in Pisa, they don't lean much at all."

I had to agree with my uncle's attitude. Let the towers lean if they want. Enjoy things the way they are. After all, it was all relative.

My House

Venice had many awful pizza restaurants, but there were a few good ones as well. Ae Oche, Tre Archi, Vesuvio, and Ristorante Casa Mia were some of our favorites.

In Cannaregio, on a side alley just off Strada Nova sits a little restaurant called Casa Mia. Frequented by Venetians, we found their service friendly and the pizza authentic. One of their specialties was a gorgonzola pizza. In the United States, most of the gorgonzola cheese available for purchase is *piccante*, similar to a strong blue cheese. In northern Italy, the milder *dolce* is more popular and is frequently used on pizzas.

Once a week, we visited Ristorante Casa Mia. Sofia, a small girl in her twenties with blond hair and a pleasant smile, waited on us every time. Debbie's favorite was the Parmigiana, pizza with grilled eggplant, and mine was the gorgonzola. One week I asked, "Sofia, I noticed on the menu that in addition to my favorite, there is also a basil pesto pizza. Could you please have the chef make me a gorgonzola, basil pesto pizza?"

Sofia shook her head. "I doubt that he will, but I will ask." Returning with our wine a few minutes later, Sofia confirmed, "The chef won't make it. He said to try the basil pesto pizza today instead."

This became my standing order. Each week, I would order a gorgonzola, basil pesto pizza, and Sofia would bring me one or the other, but never combined. One week, I said, "Sofia, we have been coming here every week for over three months, and never has the chef made me a gorgonzola, basil pesto pizza. If this restaurant is truly *Casa Mia*, shouldn't I be able to get the pizza I want?"

"I'll see what I can do." Sofia smiled as she walked away.

"This may be the day I finally get that pizza I've been waiting for all this time!" I told Debbie excitedly.

She chuckled, "I hope it's all you've been hoping for." The red table wine tasted even better than usual as I awaited this gastronomic delight prepared just for me.

"The chef was in a good mood today. In fact, he even chuckled a bit when he agreed to make you this gorgonzola, pesto pizza. *Ecco qua.* Here you go." Sofia placed the green and white pizza in front of me, gave Debbie her pizza parmigiana, and left. Debbie watched as I placed the first bite into my mouth. But instead of the gastronomic delight I was expecting, it was a gastronomic disaster! The basil pesto and the gorgonzola, while heavenly on separate pizzas, combined to produce an overwhelmingly strong and seemingly toxic flavor. The pizza was virtually inedible.

Debbie laughed as she ate piece after piece of her eggplant pizza while watching me trying to eat even one piece of my toxic combo. There was no way of removing either the pesto or the gorgonzola, and I gave up trying after a few minutes, only to look up and see that Sofia had returned.

Noticing that Debbie's pizza was almost entirely devoured, and mine almost untouched, Sofia asked, "*E allora, comé va?*"

"Um, for some reason I'm just not too hungry today," I replied. "Could I have a box?"

I put the pizza in its cardboard coffin, drew a skull and crossbones on the top, and upon leaving Casa Mia, deposited it in one of those culinary mausoleums on the street and walked away. Never again did I order a gorgonzola-pesto pizza, and never again did Sofia mention it.

Even when it's your house, sometimes the chef knows best.

Louis' Little Brother

Venice had its share of street vendors. There were Senegalese selling beanbag characters, Nigerians selling dancing Mickey and Minnie Mouse stick figures, and Moroccans selling designer purses. The purses were from Louis Vuitton, Dolce & Gabbana, Gucci, and many other famous designers. "How can they sell those great purses for forty dollars?" I asked.

"They're fakes," Debbie answered.

After discussing the purses with our Venetian friends, I learned that they were actually made in China in sweat shops and distributed by some unscrupulous Italians for the Moroccans to sell on the streets throughout Italy. It was, however, illegal to sell them in Venice. The Marocchini—Moroccans—however, had developed a system of evading the police. Three or four of them would lay out their purses on a blanket while one stood guard with a cell phone ready to notify the others of the arriving police. Just in time, they would dump their wares into a large bag and move a few blocks away to set up shop again. It was a fun game of cat and mouse, and I spent hours at corner cafés watching it play out.

One day, the rules changed. My morning walk brought rise to new signs posted all over the city. It seemed that, in typical Venetian logic, if the police couldn't stop the Marocchini from selling purses, then they would instead fine the tourists who purchased them.

"Warning, you could be fined €500 for purchasing counterfeit purses," the signs cautioned. Everywhere in the city—in the train station, the vaporetti, the town squares— the new signs warned tourists not to commit a crime by purchasing the evil handbags.

As I walked the city, however, it was evident the Marocchini were still there, although business was just a bit slower than usual. Over time, the warnings were less apparent, and many of the signs in the *vaporetti* returned to the normal announcements of upcoming opera performances at La Fenice. The scouts were on the corners warning the other Marocchini of the approaching police, and the cat and mouse game was back.

"Happy birthday, Deb! Look what I got for you!" I said, proudly displaying a new purse.

"You bought me a Louis Vuitton purse! How sweet!"

"Well, not exactly. It's a *Larry* Vuitton purse, from his, uh, younger brother," I said sheepishly.

"Is this purse one of those fakes from the Marocchini on the street?"

"Yes, but it was only twenty-five euro! I worked him down from forty!"

Over the course of the following week, the zipper broke, the handle came off, and one of the gold feet came undone. I carefully pieced everything together, applied super glue, and left the purse on the table in the foyer. "Leave it right here, Debbie. When people enter the apartment, they will see your beautiful Larry Vuitton purse. Just don't let anyone touch it!

About a week later, taking Debbie out for dinner, I noticed that she was using the Larry Vuitton purse I had repaired. "So, you decided to use it after all, even though it's fake?" I chuckled.

"Oh, no. I threw that piece of junk out and visited his older brother at the Louis Vuitton boutique. But like you, I got a bargain. This purse was originally four thousand euro, but was on sale for twenty-five hundred! I knew you wanted me to have one, so I went ahead and bought it! Thanks for the birthday present!"

As we sat in the restaurant, the Marocchini outside were selling their wares to unsuspecting tourists.

Men, be aware when travelling to Venice. Far more costly than the €500 fine is the possibility that your wife may purchase the real thing!

The Ghetto

"Today we will take a different path back to the apartment," Gastone said as we left the *Torrefazione* after having finished our coffee and brioche. "I want to show you the Ghetto." He seemed on a mission, wanting to share something important with me.

"Look up. Did you notice that these buildings here in the Ghetto are the tallest in Venice? Not only are they tall, but each floor has low ceilings, some only six feet high. This allowed the Jews to house more people on this small island to which they were confined." Indeed, the floors seemed very close, apparently built when people were shorter than they are now.

"Our own apartment building was the tallest in Venice," he continued. "In fact, from our rooftop, the Venetians could see Napoleon's troop movements back on the mainland. So Napoleon had the top floor of the building removed."

"Do you see that doorway, just to the right of the pet store? Read to me the inscription over the door," Gastone demanded.

"Banco Rosso—Red Bench," I replied, intrigued. "But what does it mean, Gastone?"

"Centuries ago at this point, a bench, or 'banco,' was set up. This was the Red Bank. You see, banking was one of the few professions in which the Jews were allowed to engage, and they did so at a bench outside. In fact, one of the benches was set up right here. Your English word 'Bank' comes from 'banco,' or bench. If a banker engaged in illegal loans or other nefarious activity, the police would break his bench, symbolizing the end of his business. A broken bench is a 'banco rotto' in Italian, which became the word 'bankrupt' you still use in English to this day!"

Gastone was on a roll. "Before Napoleon's rule, Christian guards controlled the exits to the Ghetto. Napoleon did away with the guards and built this iron bridge leading off of the Ghetto." We walked past the Jewish bakery and the Jewish bookstore, and arrived at the ground-floor door to our apartment building.

"No, not yet," he said, tugging at my arm. "Just a few more feet. Here, look at these." Gastone let go of my arm to point to holes in the walls of the passageway to Rio Cannaregio. "Here, five meters from our apartment door, is where the gates used to be, keeping the Jews inside at night and during Christian holidays. Living in our apartment back in the seventeenth and eighteenth centuries, you would not have had the same freedom to come and go as you do today." I gulped. Our apartment door was on the inside of the Ghetto gates.

Since Gastone was so talkative, as we walked through the door and up the five steps to our apartment elevator, I asked, "Gastone, why doesn't our elevator go all the way down to the ground floor? Why was it installed such that we have to walk up five steps to get to the elevator landing? Wouldn't that make it difficult for someone in a wheelchair to use the elevator? And why does our building have an elevator when almost no other private buildings have one?"

As the elevator took us to Gastone's floor, he explained, "The elevator can't be placed at ground level. When *Acqua Alta* arrives, it could flood the entire elevator, so it was installed above the highest point for *Acqua Alta*. As for why we have an elevator at all, come into my apartment, and I'll explain."

I made coffee while Gastone shared the story of the elevator. "Near the end of her life, my wife was confined to a wheelchair. Without an elevator, she would have been stuck in this apartment, never again able to visit friends, to eat out, or to go to the market. She would have been a prisoner in her own home."

I recalled visions of countless elderly people in Venice having no elevator and shuffling up countless flights of stairs. And as we had previously learned, living on the ground floor was not an alternative. "So you had this elevator installed just for your wife? You must have truly loved her." Even as the words left my mouth, it seemed so silly to state something so obvious.

Gastone paused. *"Mi dispiace,"* he said, excusing himself as he wiped the tears from his eyes. I sat quietly sipping my coffee. Minutes passed before he said another word. "She only got to use the elevator a few times before... before she died."

He got up, hugged me a bit tighter than normal as he kissed me on both cheeks, and said, "Same time tomorrow, okay?" Clearly, he wanted to be alone.

For the rest of our time in Venice, that elevator was no longer just a convenient way to get to the sixth floor. It was a sign of love from one man to his wife, as important to him as was the Taj Mahal, built by an ancient emperor in memory of *his* wife.

The Museum of Eternal Restoration

On the Grand Canal, there was a beautiful *palazzo* called the *Fondago dei Turchi*. Years ago, the Turks used the palace as their market for selling grains and other goods. For two hundred years, a small mosque inside served both the Shiites and the Sunnis, living, eating, and praying under the same roof. The façade facing the Grand Canal was one of my favorites. Many of the beautiful *palazzi* were privately owned, and thus visitors didn't get to peek behind the walls. But since this *palazzo* was now the Museum of Natural History, I would have the opportunity to see the courtyard and rooms hidden inside.

The museum was directly across the Grand Canal from the San Marcuola *traghetto* ferry stop. So on a sunny morning in April, I boarded the *traghetto* and stood as the gondolier ferried me across the canal and arrived at the entrance. "Closed for Renovation until February," the sign said. But being Venice, if construction was to be finished in February, one could hope for it to be completed in June.

Each month, I checked on the progress, eagerly awaiting the reopening. One day in late June, the curator arrived while I was gazing at the door. Recognizing me from my many previous visits, he said, "Sorry, but we are still closed."

"Yes, but I have been waiting anxiously for the reopening. When will it reopen?" I asked.

The curator paused, looked around, and said, "If you will be careful of the construction, I can let you in now. We will reopen in about a week."

The curator took me into a five-by-ten room with a forty-gallon aquarium. "Animals of the Venetian Lagoon," said the sign. There were two small fish and a few snails in the tank. I found myself hoping that these were not *all* of the animals of the Venetian lagoon. We moved into the courtyard.

The courtyard was breathtaking. How amazing it would have been to watch the boats come and go, grain stacked in every corner, gold coins exchanging hands, and nightly celebrations. Today, however, there was only a murky fountain with four Koi struggling to survive. In the corner where I envisioned grain, there was a wooden canoe with three wooden monkeys inside.

"Would you like to go upstairs?" the curator asked. "The big hall is up these stairs."

"*Ma si,*" I replied. Excited, I climbed the two flights of stairs whereupon he opened the oversized door into the big hall where, there on display, was... a dinosaur. Filling the entire room, towering above me, ready to place me into its skeletal belly was the king of prehistoric creatures. I hadn't known that Venice, this land built upon millions of tree trunks pounded into the ground over a thousand years ago, was also home to dinosaurs. But there it was, right there in the grand hall. The Turks would have been proud. Yep, their grand Venetian *palazzo* was home to a total of six fish, a few snails, three wooden monkeys, and a dinosaur.

I went many times since that first visit, and happily, the museum has grown. On my most recent visit, the aquarium had a few crabs, the fountain had been cleaned, and the four Koi were thriving. The monkeys were still in their canoe, and there was an espresso vending machine near the stairs. There were dinosaur teeth as well in the grand hall, and a movie showing how the dinosaur was moved from its original home in... Africa.

Note: As I write this, I have just returned from the museum. It is once again closed for renovation.

It's a Good Law

Six months of living in Venice, and it still sometimes seemed impossible to understand the locals. *"Mi dispiace, ancora?"* I asked the young lady sitting on the park bench to explain again the leash law for dogs.

Freckles and I had been walking the new neighborhood looking for new places to pee—well, more so for Freckles than for me—when we came upon a small iron gate leading into a vast park. As with most of the parks in Venice, this one was almost hidden from view from the nearby walkway. The park was split into two sections; one side had a playground for kids, and the other had wide-open fields and a few non-functional fountains surrounded by benches. There was a sign stating that it was forbidden for dogs to be off-leash at any time, yet there were two large dogs, a gray German Shepherd and a black retriever, running from one end of the field to the other at full speed.

The young lady on the park bench was holding an empty leash in her hand. "Why don't you let your dog run free?" she asked. "Look at Lucky (pronounced *loo-key*) and Pippo playing. It's such a great day to let them run."

I sat down on the bench with Freckles at my feet. "But the sign says that dogs must be on a leash at all times."

"Yes," she responded, "it does. And it's a very good law. You see, on the other side of the park there is a playground, and it would be very bad if a dog bit one of the children. But it's such a beautiful day, and Lucky needs to run. And besides, the groundskeeper is on the other side of the park right now, so it's okay." It was a bit difficult to understand her; apparently, I still had a way to go in comprehending Venetian dialect.

Taking Freckles off of the leash so she could join Lucky and Pippo, I asked, "Are both dogs yours?"

"Oh, no, I don't own a dog. My landlord would never allow it." Seeing the confused look on my face as I looked down at the leash in her hand, she explained, "I am babysitting Lucky, the black dog. My name is Valentina, what's yours?"

"Giuseppe," I said instinctively. Watching Freckles run, I said, "It seems odd to me that you Venetians have so many laws to which no one pays attention, like this leash law."

She laughed. "Oh, I'm not Venetian. I'm from Moldavia, and without papers or a visa, this is the only work I could find. I take care of people's homes and their dogs. This has been my work for over two years. And that German shepherd, he belongs to Silvia, the lady holding a leash and standing there by the tree. She is from Dubrovnik, and she too takes care of Venetian homes and pets."

Just then, the groundskeeper approached our bench. "Your dogs must be on a leash at all times. See the sign?" he said sternly before walking away, shaking his head.

Valentina smiled. "Don't worry. He says the same thing every day."

Valentina, Silvia, and I put our dogs on their leashes and left the park for a local café and more conversation. I discovered that many of the local Venetians I spoke with every day were not Venetians at all. They were part of an underground economy, people with no visas, who paid no taxes, but performed an important role in Venetian society.

Silvia tried to explain. "It's a very good law, this immigration law they have here in Italy. After all, they can't let just anyone walk in here and go to work. But we need jobs, and most Italians aren't interested in doing this work, so in the end it works out for everyone." I agreed, and as we gathered our things to leave the café, I noticed an article in the newspaper on the counter: *Mayor of Verona says that the autostrada speed limit is "merely a suggestion."* I could almost hear him say, "It's a good law, but..."

It's a Dog's Life

Debbie had settled into her daily routine. After taking Freckles to the park for a walk in the morning, she took her to the Grand Canal, where both would get in a *traghetto* and, standing with five or ten other locals, they would cross the canal and get out at the Rialto market. At the Rialto, Debbie could buy fresh seafood, fruits, vegetables, mushrooms, cheese, and meats. Butcher shops lined the edge of the market, with turkeys, chicken, and wild birds hanging in the windows with their heads and feathers still firmly attached. Large rounds of cheese sat alongside ricotta so fresh that steam emanated from the plates.

"Freckles," the butcher cried out. "*Vien qua*. Come here, I've been waiting for you." Freckles, too, had been waiting, and eagerly devoured the chunks of mortadella the butcher saved for her.

At Debbie's favorite produce table, the vendor picked out the ripest San Marzano tomatoes, to be used in making sauce that evening, while the man at the corner booth shouted the benefits of his artichoke hearts. At the spice table, the old man belted out opera, stopping only long enough to tell jokes to friends passing by,

Arms full of freshness from heaven, Debbie once again boarded the *traghetto* with Freckles between her feet, crossed the canal and returned home. As I joined her, coming home from the daily ritual with the boys, wonderful aromas fill the apartment as she experimented with the day's market finds.

Dogs played an important role in the lives of Venetians. Man's best friends followed their owners everywhere on the island. Dogs could frequently be seen on the *vaporetti* buses, the *traghetti*, in the market, inside restaurants, and even on the trains heading out of town. There was even an old Venetian story about a spaniel named Sol. It seemed that Sol's owner, a senator, lived in Campo Santo Stefano, but Sol preferred the life in Dorsoduro, on the other side of the Grand Canal. Each day, Sol would leave his home and head down to the *traghetto* crossing at Santa Maria del Giglio. The gondoliers knew the dog and would allow him to board and cross with them. After enjoying the day in Dorsoduro, Sol would return by *traghetto*, crossing the Grand Canal again, and head home. Hearing his dog bark at the bottom of the stairs, the senator would let Sol back into the house. Once a week, the senator settled with the gondoliers and paid Sol's fare.

As spring was ending, Debbie and I had taken on the rhythm of Venetian life, and could understand Sol's love of life here in Venice. Why anyone would ever leave this paradise was certainly beyond me.

8

VIVALDI'S INFERNO

Under Pressure

Venice was founded in the fifth century. Many of the *palazzi* were built around the twelfth century, by my calculations roughly two or three years before modern plumbing.

Our apartment, however, had all the modern conveniences, such as hot and cold running water. As in many apartments, there was no real water heater, just a gas flame, which heated the water as we used it. The flame was controlled by a valve in the pipe that measured the flow of water passing through it. When the hot water tap was turned on, the water flowed through the pipe, signaling for the flame to start. The flame heated the pipe, and therefore the water, and the hot water exited the faucet, thus improving the lives of the humans living there. Sort of.

When washing dishes, this concept worked well. But the bathroom pipes had become corroded over the centuries, and the shower had very little water coming out of the showerhead, not enough, in fact, to trigger the little flame designed to improve my life by providing hot water. The water to the tub was sufficient to start the flame, but the shower couldn't. I disliked baths. And besides, with the lack of water pressure, drawing the bath took almost thirty minutes. And the tub was so small, my legs never seemed to fit. A bath was, therefore, not my idea of relaxation. But spending the remaining time in Venice taking cold showers wasn't that appealing, either.

The landlord had a simple solution. "Just turn on the sink faucet in the bathroom when you take a shower. The combination of both the shower and the sink will pull enough water through the system to cause the heater flame to start, giving you a hot shower."

"Why didn't I think of that?" I thought. "If you want a hot shower, let the hot water run in the bathroom sink!"

Over the months, the sink-shower strategy worked well. But over time, we found it necessary to have the kitchen faucet running as well as the bathroom sink, in order to keep the shower hot. When houseguests spent the night, it took a coordinated effort to ensure hot showers. Admittedly, I was afraid to put up much of a fuss out of fear that our landlord might hire the plumber/electrician from Santa Croce, who would be likely to close off the shower entirely, claiming it to somehow be the source of the problem.

As the summer approached, cold showers gave welcome relief to the hot days and warm nights. Who needed hot showers, anyway?

Summer was hot in Venice. The humidity ran around ninety percent, the temperature hung in the high eighties or low nineties, and there was virtually no air conditioning anywhere except in the five-star hotels. As May turned into June, we noticed the elderly residents leaving to spend the summer in the mountains. Shopping was becoming a chore, as there was no relief from the heat. Out of necessity, we adapted to the Venetian time schedule—up early to shop, back inside with the windows open but the shutters closed from noon until three-thirty, then finishing errands after dark.

I could only imagine how difficult it must have been for Antonio Vivaldi to concentrate on writing music in

Venice's intense summer heat. It was no wonder that in his masterpiece, "The Four Seasons," summer seemed to take on a more violent tone.

In the evenings, we slept with the windows open, hoping for a small breeze. Then came the mosquitoes. First, we slept with our faces under the sheets to hide from them, then we purchased the ubiquitous "*Vape*," nighttime mosquito killers. The "*Vape*" unit was a small device that plugged into an electric outlet, and emitted some sort of poison into the air to kill the mosquitoes. It worked well, but each morning we woke up with sore throats, wondering what long-term effects these devices were having on our reproductive systems.

Four important facts about summer in Venice:

It is very hot.

The humidity is high.

There are tons of mosquitoes.

There are very few window screens.

One day in a hardware store, I saw a do-it-yourself, instant window screen kit. It was a sheet of screen and about twenty feet of Velcro stripping with glue on one side. I came home, installed the Velcro strips and attached the screen. Voila! In ten minutes, I had solved the mosquito problem forever! Only nineteen windows to go. I was so proud, I called Debbie in to see my work.

"That's great, but now how do I get to the clothesline?"

There were very few clothes dryers in Venice, since the average apartment had only a 3,500 watt circuit, less than what was needed for a space heater and a hair dryer at the same time. The clothesline, therefore, was a very important item in the everyday life of a Venetian.

"It's simple." I demonstrated. "Just pull on the screen here, and the Velcro will...." At that moment, the entire assembly came down. The plaster on the buildings crumbled easily due to the humidity, and the plaster came off the window along with the Velcro strips. That night, we slept under the sheets again.

Back at the hardware store the next morning, I discussed the problem with Filippo, the owner. "Yes, the plaster coming off is a problem with those cheap kits. But we also sell these permanent screens. They work just like blinds. Give them a tug, and they roll up so you can get to the clothesline outside your window. Then, pull them down for a tight seal to keep the mosquitoes out at night. We can have them installed tomorrow for seventy euro per window." With twenty windows in our rental apartment and only five months left in Venice, I opted to install the screens on half the windows and keep the others closed at night. As expensive as it was, I had no choice.

In just two short weeks, a young man from the hardware store installed the screens. Sure enough, we could keep them open during the day and pull them down at night.

We slept well that first night, until about two o'clock in the morning when we were awakened by a loud "Thump—flap, flap, flap—crash!" One of the screens in the bedroom had come up on its own, allowing those miniature vampires into the apartment. The vibration sent our basil plant off the windowsill to crash into pieces once again in our neighbor's courtyard. The remainder of the night, we slept under the sheets again.

Over time, we adjusted the screens to stay open during the day and closed at night. I stood by my window one evening feeling the breeze and marveling at these screens, which allowed us access to the clothesline but also gave protection from the mosquitoes at night.

It was then that I saw one of my shirts blow off the clothesline, land in the canal, and float away like a gondola on its way home.

Bled

"Oh, my God! Is this heat ever going to end?" I heard Debbie exclaim. She was standing at the sink in shorts and a t-shirt, with a cold washcloth on her forehead. "I've taken three showers today, and it's only two in the afternoon. Look at me! I'm already dripping in sweat!" July had brought temperatures over a hundred degrees during the day, dropping only to the high eighties at night. With no air conditioning, we were miserable day and night. We had to find relief somewhere. There were no malls on the island and very few other spots where someone could get out of the heat. While some of the Italians headed to the beach, most of our friends had disappeared to their summer homes in the Dolomites. Misurina, a small mountain resort in northern Italy was full in the summer with people hiking, swimming in the mountain lakes, or just enjoying the cool mountain air.

But Debbie had been reading about Slovenia, just northeast of Italy. "Let's rent an air-conditioned car and go to Bled, in Slovenia. I read that the town of Bled has a beautiful lake, too. Just get me out of this hellhole!" Debbie reserved a rental car, making certain it was air conditioned, while I searched the internet for an air-conditioned hotel on Lake Bled. Debbie went ahead to Piazzale Roma to get the rental car, and I followed behind with the luggage, six bottles of cold water, and Freckles. With everything in the car, and the air conditioning on full force, Debbie paused before hitting the road. "This is heaven!" she exclaimed. "We could just stay right here, in this car until fall."

About thirty minutes outside of Venice, traffic heading north came to a halt. Evidently, we weren't the only ones escaping the city heat. But it just didn't matter as long as we had *air conditioning.*

As we reached the border between Italy and Slovenia, I asked, "What language do they speak in Slovenia, Slovenian?"

"How the hell should I know?" came the reply. I sifted through my travel guidebooks, but none of them even mentioned Slovenia.

When we reached the border, the heat filled the car as we rolled down the window to hand our passports to the border guard. "How can it be so hot out there? The thermometer says thirty-two degrees." I reminded her that thirty-two Celsius equaled roughly ninety degrees Fahrenheit. The border guard reviewed our passports carefully, then let us pass without saying a word. We returned to our air-conditioned cocoon and finished our drive to Bled.

The view from the hotel grounds was stunning. Covered in flowering vines, it overlooked Lake Bled with a clear view of the castle towering over the lake from the other side. In the center of the lake was a small island with what appeared to be a small church rising from the shoreline.

The receptionist handed us the keys to our room. "I've given you one of our best suites," she said in Italian. "It has a great view of the lake and is surrounded by flowers."

As I carried the luggage up the stairs and into the room, I heard Debbie say, "Oh, honey, come here and look!" She was on the terrace surrounded by purple flowers, enjoying the view of the lake.

I rushed out to enjoy the view, but retreated quickly to the room. It seemed that we were not the only ones enjoying the flowering vines. A swarm of bees had moved in, and they were not willing to share the terrace. We quickly closed the doors to the terrace. As the windows had no screens, we closed them as well, after shooing the last bee out of the room. We turned to the air conditioner for comfort. But alas, the air conditioner didn't work. A call to the hotel receptionist brought a ten-inch fan to the room. Sweating inside our hotel room, we chuckled about how hot it was back in Venice, and how it was almost ten degrees cooler here in Bled, closed up in our hotel room fourteen hundred feet above sea level.

"We can't stay in the hotel room all day. Let's go down to the lake," Debbie suggested. Passing by the front desk, I borrowed a guide to Slovenia written in English. While Debbie, Freckles, and I walked alongside the lakeshore, I perused my new travel guidebook.

"In the center of the lake is a church dedicated to the goddess of love and fertility. There is a tradition," I read aloud, "of the man rowing his bride to the church to show his love."

"That sounds like a great tradition," Debbie said, as she handed a few thousand *Tolar*, the Slovenian currency, to the boy renting the rowboats to eager tourists. I could barely see the church roughly three quarters of a mile away in the center of the lake.

We loaded the rowboat with Debbie, Freckles, and two liters of water. Tall trees lined most of the lakeshore, and snow-capped mountains towered in the distance. "What a gorgeous view, just look at the castle!" Debbie exclaimed during one of the periods when I had stopped to drench myself both inside and out with water.

"Heck with the castle," I gasped. "Let me know when you see a tugboat." I went back to rowing. The town was getting smaller, and it appeared that the island might be getting closer.

When we finally reached the shore of the small island containing the church, I paused again for water, and once more read my travel guide. "There are ninety-nine steps up to the church. Traditionally, the groom carries his bride up the steps. During the trip the bride must remain silent." I chuckled.

"Who needs tradition anyway?" she asked, rushing up the steps. "You had better hurry up, there's a storm coming in." I recalled a story of a hillside in Normandy called the "Hillside of Two Lovers." The legend said the King had mandated any suitor wishing to marry his daughter would have to carry her up the entire length of the hill. One young man finally did, but then collapsed and died. Distressed, the young lady threw herself off of the hill onto the rocks below. I was glad to see Debbie making the trip up the hill on her own power.

After a quick trip up the ninety-nine steps and a stop for a glass of water, we headed back. Admittedly, the trip back was cooler due to the rainstorm, but I was concerned the boat might fill up with water before we returned. In the end, my plan to use my empty two-liter bottle to bail my tiny craft wasn't necessary. We returned the rowboat, and I collapsed in the hotel room.

Debbie opened the terrace doors. Happily, the bees had moved on, possibly finding other tourists to terrorize. We were free to enjoy our terrace. Looking out over the lake far in the distance, we could see the island with the church rising from the center, taunting other tourists into cardiac arrest from demonstrating their love to their future widows by carting them across the lake in a small rowboat before carrying them up the ninety-nine steps.

"By the way, what is the name of that church?" Debbie asked.

"The Church of the Immaculate Heart Attack," I quipped.

The next day, we drove through Triglav National Park, the only national park in Slovenia. It was a lush mountainous park with fields full of flowers, one restaurant, a lifetime supply of sheep blocking the roads, and breathtaking drops visible from the narrow winding roads. But nothing took our breath away like the Slovenian-Italian border station.

As we left Slovenia traveling through the back roads, we arrived at the border between Slovenia and Italy. Upon leaving Slovenia, the Slovenian guard checked our passports, peered into the car at Freckles, and waved us on. We drove the twenty feet to the Italian border station where the Italian police looked at our passports, conversed with each other, and said, "You can't come in. Go back to Slovenia." They handed us our passports and went back inside the station.

We couldn't go back to Italy? Was it the dog? Did they know we didn't have visas? Would we spend the rest of our lives in this twenty feet between Slovenia and Italy?

Debbie got out of the car and knocked on the window of the Italian border station. "Why can't we come into Italy?" she asked.

"Your passport is not from the European Union," came the reply. You must take the autostrada into Italy where you will be checked by the larger border station. Out here in the country, we are only equipped for EU passports."

Relieved, we returned to Slovenia. This time, the Slovenian police studied our passports carefully. "If Italy doesn't want them, why should we?" they must have been thinking. Finally, the Slovenian police waved us back into their country. An hour later, we crossed the border into

Italy, but this time on the autostrada. The Italian police glanced at the covers of our passports and waved us in.

A slight breeze came through the window when we returned to our apartment in Venice. With no flowering vines, no bees, and no churches in the middle of the lake beckoning, we sat on the couch exhausted from our trip to the not-so-frigid region of Slovenia.

Destruction on the Amalfi Coast

It was another warm day in Venice, and Debbie wanted to head to the beach. She had visited the Amalfi coast on the east side of Italy, south of Rome, with our relatives, and wanted to return to show me her favorite cliff-side restaurants, beaches, and the Isle of Capri. Valentina, the Moldavian girl I had met in the park, agreed to watch Freckles for the weekend.

We left the next morning, taking the train to Naples, then renting a two-seater Fiat for the ride to the coast. Roberto, the manager of the rental car office, picked us up at the train station. "I picked out a special car just for the two of you. You are going to love this car. It's a brand new Fiat, and it has all the latest features. It just came in yesterday." Dropping us off at the car, he opened the door for Debbie, closed it, and smiled. "Have a great weekend, and enjoy the car!" He waved as we drove off. Pulling out of the lot, the odometer registered only forty-five kilometers.

Our friends, Agata Lima and her daughter Chiara, had invited us to their home for dinner. Mamma Agata was quite the chef, having cooked for Sophia Loren, Fred Astaire, Jacqueline Kennedy, Pierce Brosnan, and quite a few other celebrities. So it was an opportunity we couldn't turn down. Out of respect, we planned our trip to be sure we arrived on time.

Having driven the Pacific Coast Highway in California, as well as the hairpin turns on the Cinque Terra roads in Italy, I thought the Amalfi coast would be a piece of cake.

"Would you like me to drive?" Debbie asked, as we left Naples.

"No thanks, I'll be fine," I assured her. After passing the coastal town of Sorrento, an odd thing happened. The coastal road shrunk to two very skinny lanes, one of which always seemed to be occupied by a large tour bus.

"Are you okay?" Debbie asked.

"I'm fine, why?"

"Well, your knuckles are white, your top speed has been thirty five, and there's a line of cars behind us."

"Don't worry," I explained. "By driving slow, I'm protecting them from going over the cliff." Just then, I slammed on the brakes.

Around the curves, and it seemed like the entire road was nothing but curves, there were mirrors strategically positioned so that you could see the bus around the corner just before it pushed you over the edge! The curves were so narrow that if a bus was taking one, there was no room for even the smallest car coming in the other direction. So, the drive was a series of stops before the curves because there was always a bus coming, and I would need to stop and catch my breath.

Finally, we arrived at the town of Ravello with minutes to spare. "Just turn right at the curve in the road, and we are on the left," Chiara instructed by phone. "See you in a few minutes."

When the next curve in the road arrived, we turned right as instructed and arrived in the Ravello town square. It looked a lot like a pedestrian-only zone, but following Chiara's instructions, I looked for their home on the left. The first thing visible on the left was a little old man on a bench. I stopped to look around, and without saying a word, the old man pointed the way with his cane. "I guess Mamma Agata gets a lot of visitors," I chuckled. The left turn took me onto a one-lane road barely wider than our car. Both sides of the road had rock walls, and it appeared to get skinnier and skinnier. After about fifty feet, we pulled in our side mirrors.

"Are you sure this is the right way?" Debbie asked.

"The old man surely wouldn't lie."

It was then that I heard the crunching sound of grinding metal. We were scraping the rock wall on both sides of the car. The car was stuck. Debbie said nothing. Crawling out of the driver's window, I analyzed the situation. The road continued to get smaller, and the only vehicles I saw ahead were motorcycles. A crowd of tourists and residents alike had gathered. People were taking photographs of the car, literally stuck between a rock and a hard place. The old man with the cane stopped by to take a look, shook his head, and stepped back without uttering a word.

I climbed back into the driver's seat and cried. Debbie put her hand on my shoulder. Clearly, we would inflict even more damage to the car if we were to back up, but we had no choice. I put the car into reverse. The tourists fled, and the old man returned to his bench. The grinding sound stopped, and we were finally free. Leaving the town square, we retraced our steps back up the hill and started over. We came down the hill and made our first right, winding up face to face again with the wicked old man. I resisted the urge to press the gas pedal and called Chiara instead. "Not that turn, the next one," she replied. "So sorry about your car!"

We arrived an hour late for lunch. With Chiara and Mamma Agata looking at the damaged car, all was forgiven. Mamma Agata was truly a spectacular chef, and her daughter was following in her footsteps quite well. We laughed, cried, ate, drank limoncello, and laughed some more. After our wonderful meal of *pappardelle*, chicken with sage, lasagna with smoked mozzarella, and her signature lemon torte, we toured their garden and enjoyed the sunset from their backyard terrace.

After dark, the damage to the car was less noticeable. I tugged to open the driver's door, smiled a weak smile as Debbie got in, and pushed hard to close it.

For the remainder of our time on the Amalfi coast, Debbie drove. We averaged sixty to seventy kilometers per hour around the turns, and Debbie became quite good at passing those silly tourists who drove so slowly.

With our weekend over, we returned the car to the rental agency in Naples. Roberto greeted us in the office. "How was it? Don't you just love that car?" We walked outside for the inspection. Debbie explained to Roberto about the road, the rock walls, and the grinding sound as we got stuck. Roberto's face dropped. It was as if he had lost a good friend.

I waited outside while Debbie filled out the insurance papers. While driving us back to the train station, Roberto said nothing.

On the train back to Venice, we envisioned Roberto having dinner with his wife that night, discussing the dumb Americans who had destroyed his car. Debbie and I thought it best to choose a different rental company for our next Amalfi Coast adventure.

Bay Leaves

I was out and about in Venice one morning watching the many graduation rituals throughout the town. Evidently, the college graduate was paraded around town in short shorts, a clown outfit, or a dress—for men. A large wreath was placed on their head, and they were required to read something their friends had written on a large scroll. While I was trying to understand these impromptu ceremonies, Debbie called and asked me to pick up a bay leaf from the store on my way home. She would be cooking a roast that night, and the bay leaf was important, so I was instructed not to forget this precious culinary ingredient.

My best chance for obtaining a bay leaf was at the supermarket Coop, I thought. Checking their entire selection of five spices, I found no bay leaves. A search in the fruits and vegetables section discovered basil and rosemary, but still no bay leaves. I returned home empty-handed. That afternoon, Debbie went out on a search of her own. The *fruttivendoli* selling produce at the street market didn't have any, and neither did the fruit and vegetable store, nor the deli. A trip to the second deli brought no bay leaves, but Debbie did come home with an explanation. It seemed that many people had bay bushes in their gardens, and that was where they got bay leaves. Since we were the only people we knew with a garden, and since our garden didn't have any bay bushes, we postponed making the roast until the next day.

Debbie did make one additional attempt to acquire a bay leaf that evening. She left the house with the intention of going straight to the spice store, Màscari, near the Rialto Bridge. They tended to have every type of spice one would need. But alas, no trip in that direction could occur without stopping along the way to see Gino and his pastries. With the spice store having closed before Debbie's arrival, she too returned home empty-handed.

The next morning on the way to Gino's pastry shop, I stopped at a different supermarket, where I found a spice jar with small pieces of bay leaves, *lauro*. After purchasing the jar and showing it to my wife, I learned that bay leaves give the dish flavor, and then must be removed before serving, or some poor unfortunate soul would be chewing on a bay leaf, which has roughly the same consistency as a dried leaf from an oak tree. My pieces of bay leaves would be impossible to remove, and therefore were rendered useless. A quick trip to the butcher shop brought no new results. The butcher knew what *lauro* leaves were, but had no idea where to get them.

Exasperated, I explained my quest to Gino. He laughed and said that the wreaths that the graduates were wearing all around town to celebrate their "laureate" degrees were made from bay leaves, and that every florist in town had plenty of them. I ran to the florist next door to the butcher shop and asked the florist for bay leaves. He handed me an entire branch free of charge and chuckled as I ran out the door with enough bay leaves to make a wreath.

We had a tasty roast that night, and to celebrate our accomplishment, I wore the wreath during dinner.

Walk With Me

One morning when I showed up at Gastone's apartment, he was carrying a small overnight bag when he answered the door. "Walk with me," was his only greeting. He handed me his bag without saying a word and walked to the *vaporetto* stop. He punched a ticket for each of us, and we found two seats together on the boat.

"The doctor says that I need to go to the hospital for treatments so that I can breathe better. My lungs are closing up, and every six months or so, I go in for treatments. I'll be gone for about two weeks. It's a long way; don't bother coming to visit me."

The private hospital, Ospedale Fatebenefratelli, was located in Cannaregio on the edge of the island near the Madonna dell'Orto church. It was a very small facility, but it had a nice park on the water.

"From this hospital, one has a perfect view of the cemetery. It's quite an incentive to get well soon," Gastone said, chuckling. Looking out I could see the island of

San Michele, the cemetery where most Venetians were temporarily buried. "Temporarily," because after twelve years, the corpses are dug up and moved to make room for new arrivals.

Over the course of the next two weeks, I visited Gastone almost every day. We would walk downstairs to the hospital café and have an espresso before settling down on a park bench to stare out into the water without saying a word. He wasn't fond of the food at the hospital, so I kept him supplied with brioche and Debbie's lasagna and manicotti.

One morning when I arrived at the hospital, Gastone was packing. "They said I can go home now." I grabbed his bag, punched two tickets for the *vaporetto*, and we headed home. As the vaporetto passed San Michele, I was thankful that the cemetery had not acquired my friend as another twelve-year visitor.

The next morning when I arrived at his apartment, we left for coffee and continued our lives as if the past two weeks had never happened.

A Discreet Little Plaque

Debbie and I decided to take a trip into the cool Italian mountains. The lady at the train station in Venice informed me that Cortina d'Ampezzo was only a few hours away by train, and had a wonderful view of the Dolomites. There was a direct train that took two hours and twenty minutes to get to Pieve di Cadore, then there was a bus waiting at the train station that finished the trip to Cortina; in another twenty minutes, we would be there.

At seven o'clock on Sunday morning, we got on the train heading north. About an hour into the trip, after the train stopped in Conegliano, we noticed the train wasn't leaving.

"Trenta minuti in ritardo," the conductor said, as he passed by. We would be thirty minutes late. When we finally arrived at Pieve di Cadore, our connection point for the bus, at ten o'clock, I ran out front to see an empty parking lot with no bus. Back inside, the lady at the information counter said there would be a bus leaving in about a half an hour, and that the ride to Cortina d'Ampezzo was a "short hour."

The bus driver greeted everyone with a hearty "*Buongiorno.*" In fact, it seemed like he knew everyone in the small hill towns. As he made his way around the winding mountain roads, he waved at all of his friends, sometimes with both hands!

In one small town, our driver saw someone he knew standing outside a café. "Come with me, let's chat! I'll bring you back in a little while," he said as his friend boarded the bus and sat right behind him. They must have been good friends because they immediately struck up an intense conversation that required every bit of the driver's concentration along with both of his hands. We were making a hairpin turn as he told his friend that he was "washing my hands of the situation," making the proper hand gestures at the same time.

When we arrived at Cortina around noon, I wanted to say "*Arrivederci*" to the driver, but thought better of it when I looked up and saw the sign that said, "Do not talk to the driver."

Cortina d'Ampezzo was a ski town in the beautifully jagged Dolomites Mountains, which hosted the winter Olympics in 1956. The Olympic ski jump was visible as we approached the town, and it appeared to be a town with many affluent visitors. We didn't have the opportunity to find out, as we were almost the only people in town with the exception of a busload of German tourists also there for the day.

Three restaurants and one bar were open. Everything else was closed. Even during the middle of a Florida hurricane, I had never seen a town so abandoned. We looked at the church bell tower from every angle. We admired the "Closed until December" signs in the store windows. We walked down the stairs to the town square. We walked back up the stairs. It was one in the afternoon. We thought about the long trip home.

The two o'clock bus stopped frequently and picked up teenage girls who all seemed to know each other. But where were the boys? Why were there only girls on the bus? The bus dropped us off back at the train station. Unfortunately, we would be waiting an hour and a half for the next train back to Venice.

The station was at the bottom of a hill with nothing around it other than winding mountain roads heading up into the clouds. I visited the café inside the station, but it was closed due to renovation. Debbie settled down in the waiting room and opened her book while I decided to find some coffee. "Two short minutes uphill," the bus driver, still standing outside, said when I asked him the location of the nearest café. Up the hill I went.

It was a skinny mountain road with no sidewalks, a mountain on one side, and a concrete fence on the other. What appeared to be dog poop lined the side of the road with the fence. I walked uphill for ten long minutes and reached the café. It was a typical neighborhood café/bar with a TV perched on top of a Coca-Cola cooler at a height of about six feet. Sitting inside the café must have been all the men and boys in the town. There were fifteen or twenty, all with their eyes glued to a soccer game.

I kept my eyes glued to the soccer match while drinking my coffee, so as not to look out of place. Debbie had asked me to get her a Coke, so I walked over to the Coke cooler with the glass door and pulled on the left side to open it. The TV shook, and the cooler didn't open. I pulled on the right side, the TV shook again, but the cooler still didn't open. After trying the left side again, I started fearing for my life should the TV fall at such a critical time during the match, and finally left the café without the Coke.

While walking downhill back to the train station, two cars were racing uphill. I glued myself to the concrete wall and realized that the poop I saw might have been from frightened tourists like me trying to make their way downhill!

Back at the train station, a sign told the history of the station. Built in 1913, the station and the rail lines it served were used to support the war effort. A "discreet little plaque" it said, "hangs on the façade in honor of the USA, which liberated Europe." Standing in front of the building, I looked for the plaque, but found nothing. As I was going over the building with a fine-toothed comb, my wife appeared.

"What are you doing?" she asked.

"I'm looking for a discreet little plaque. Help me find it." We searched the outside of the building.

"What's the plaque for?"

"You'll know when you see it, but it's really nice." We searched the inside of the building and wound up back out front by the information sign.

"Hmm, I wonder where it is," Debbie said. We searched the entire station again.

"I know it's discreet," I said, "but this is ridiculous."

When we finally boarded the train, I put my head out the window. "What on earth are you looking at?" Debbie said.

"If I wanted to thank the Americans, I would put the plaque in a place where they would see it when they arrived by train. Therefore, if I look out this window, I'll probably see it." No plaque.

As the train pulled away from the station on the long journey home, I took comfort in knowing that the "discreet little plaque" was probably hanging in the train station's closed café, right there above the TV that was certainly on top of the drink cooler. Each time the home team scored, the residents of this little town would cheer for their team, giving a little thanks to the Americans who had freed Europe.

9

MY FELLOW VENETIANS

As our time in Venice continued, we adapted to the rhythm of this city built upon water. We slowed our pace, observing the people around us.

I'm Italian

One evening, I joined my wife and daughter Stephanie at a local restaurant, "Pane, Vino, and San Daniele." The restaurant was part of a small chain which focused on the simplicity of bread, wine, and prosciutto from San Daniele, a small town north of Venice. William, the owner who was from Rome, toasted us with a glass of Prosecco. A young man and woman from Venice joined the conversation.

As the night progressed, Stephanie asked if she could take a picture with the couple. The young man jumped up, put his arm around Stephanie, and tossed the camera to his girlfriend to take a picture.

"You can't do that," she said. "We're engaged."

His response: "Yes, I can. I'm Italian!"

Hanging on by a Thread

It was a brisk sunny morning. The seven o'clock bells had finished ringing only minutes earlier as I entered the square. The only person there was the garbage man wheeling his cart and whistling the theme from *The Godfather*. The tune echoed between the church walls and the apartment buildings lining Campo San Giacomo dell'Orio.

Turning the corner into an alley, I saw an elderly lady leaning out of her third-story apartment to drop a wicker basket on a string to her friend below. The friend put a loaf of fresh bread in the basket, and it was pulled back up, disappearing into the window.

On the next *calle*, there was a familiar scene. Each day, the mailman rang the doorbell of this home, and the old man dropped a rope out the upstairs window with a clip on the end. The mail was placed on the clip, and the rope was hoisted up. There was a very large elderly population in Venice, and in any way their neighbors could help, they did.

The Sweepers

Venice was a city of alleys, small alleys that could get dirty from the remnants of junk mail laid on doorsteps as well as trash carried about by the brisk winds whipping through the alleys.

Many residents took it upon themselves to sweep the area in front of their homes each day. It was no surprise to me to see a neighbor sweeping in front of her home. A closer look revealed, however, that she was merely sweeping the trash across the alley in front of her neighbor's front door. From a practical standpoint, that didn't make much sense. The alley wasn't much wider than I am tall. Certainly, the trash would be back on her side before the day was out.

About an hour later as I exited my apartment, my suspicions were confirmed. The trash was in fact moving back to her side, being pushed there by the broom of the lady living across the alley!

The Sandwich

Stopping in a delicatessen/bread store as I walked home, I noticed a whole log of my favorite deli meat, mortadella, roughly four feet long and a foot in diameter in the window. Above it hung a movie poster, where Sophia

Loren was straddling a mortadella of the same size. After pausing to wonder if this was indeed the same fortunate meat depicted in the photo, I returned to the task at hand and told the shopkeeper that I wanted to buy some bread to make a sandwich when I get home.

"What kind of a sandwich are you going to make?" he asked.

"I have some mortadella and some soppressata at home," I responded.

"No," he said.

"What do you mean, no?"

"You should cut the bread in half, make a mortadella sandwich, then make a soppressata sandwich."

"But why?"

"Look at me," he said, pointing to all of his pre-made sandwiches. "I make sandwiches all day. I know! And you should have a glass of nice red wine, too."

"One glass of wine for the two sandwiches?" I asked.

"No. One glass with the mortadella, and one with the soppressata. Then come back tomorrow and let me know how it was."

Later that evening after dinner, I passed by his shop after visiting Carlo at Gelateria Alaska for a cup of the best pear gelato in Venice.

"Well, how were the sandwiches and wine?" the shopkeeper yelled out the door of his store.

"Perfect!" I yelled back, in between bites of gelato.

"*Bravissimo!*" he exclaimed.

I walked home enjoying my gelato and savoring the people of Venice along the way.

The Garbage Nail

Returning from Gino's *pasticceria*, "Il Bucintoro," wiping the crumbs of his apricot-filled brioche from my lips, I saw an old man outside the apartment next to mine putting a three-by-five card on a nail outside his front door. The card said, "Reserved." What could he be reserving the nail for? I had lived there just long enough to know.

There were no outside garbage cans in Venice as we had back in the suburbs in Florida, and the nearest public dumpster was two bridges away. The Venetians, however, had devised an efficient method of disposing of their garbage. Each morning, the homeowner placed the small sack from his or her kitchen garbage can on a hook attached to their front door. That kept the garbage from being blown into the canals by the wind. On some doors where this wasn't possible, a nail was hammered into the wall outside.

The garbage service came every morning with a cart on wheels, picked the bag off of everyone's door, then took the cart to the edge of the canal where the garbage boat awaited. The garbage boat picked up the cart with a crane, releasing the trap door on the bottom of the cart, thus emptying the garbage into the hull of the boat. The crane then closed the trap door and returned the cart to land.

Well, someone had been using this man's nail for their garbage! He inquired if it had been me, since I was new, whereupon I assured him it was not, as I had my very own hook, and showed it to him. He apologized, lamenting the fact that someone would use his nail for *their* garbage. For a time, we speculated as to what miscreant might have placed their plastic bag full of garbage on his private nail. I agreed that it was a shame, and entered my apartment. In retrospect, I should have offered to let him use my hook.

Wine on Tap

Around the corner from our apartment, on Rio Cannaregio, there was a store that always seemed to have a plastic bag full of garbage hanging from the doorknob when the store was closed. Upon closer inspection, the plastic bag was full of empty plastic water bottles.

Walking by the store when it was open, I noticed large casks of wine, each containing twenty gallons or so, lining the walls inside. Each cask had a plastic tube coming out of the top, with a device similar to a gasoline nozzle at the end.

"*Buongiorno!*" the man inside called out. "*Vino?*" Over the course of the next hour, the storeowner, Alberto, had me sample each of the wines in his store—Prosecco, Malvasia, Tocai, Merlot, and more—and explained the process of *vini alla spina*, or wines on tap. Most everyone in Venice drank bottled water at home. When the neighbors were done with their bottles, they put them in the plastic bag on his door, or just brought them inside if the store was open. Then, when a customer walked in to purchase wine, Alberto simply filled the empty water bottles with whatever wine the customer wanted, sticking the nozzle in the water bottle, then filling and recapping it. The customer left with a liter of wine for less than two euro, sure to return the next day, hopefully with an empty bottle.

"So, you turn water into wine?" I asked.

"Well, I guess I do." He chuckled, then added, "but not the way Jesus did, of course."

Each day as I passed by the store, Alberto would call me in to show me the latest photos of his family, or just to discuss the weather, wine, and local politics.

Many times I would be passing in front of Alberto's wine store, in a hurry to return home with whatever grocery item Debbie needed for the evening meal, and I would hear Alberto say, *"Vino?"*

When a Venetian invited, it was disrespectful to say no, since what could possibly be more important than a friend who wants to talk over a glass of wine? Everything else could wait, and in Venice, it usually did.

Nighttime in Venice

Just getting off of work at eleven o'clock, I headed out to enjoy the nighttime stillness of Venice.

It amazed me that tourists typically spent one day walking from the Ponte Degli Scalzi to *Piazza San Marco* and back, thinking that they understood this city of water. In the meantime, there was a beehive of activity going on behind the façade. There were real people relaxing in their private courtyards. Beautiful parks where dogs ran free—when the guards weren't looking—and children playing just steps away from the crowd. We locals walked the back alleys, rarely even bumping into the tourists who congregated around the restaurants with menus posted in six languages. Then, at sunset, the tourists would leave, and the city was ours.

As I exited the apartment into the alley, I found two lovers in a heated embrace, completely oblivious to the piece of plaster falling from the building above, which barely missed them as it crashed to the ground and shattered into tiny pieces. Passing them, I entered the local square, Campo San Giacomo dell'Orio, where restaurants and cafés were filled with people eating outside. Music and wine flowed from every corner. I walked into a café as a young lady made a proclamation which I didn't comprehend. She bit the hand of the bartender who grimaced in mock horror as

I looked on, drinking my Prosecco. She laughed and ran out the door.

After walking further to get a slice of pizza at the next corner, I stopped to enjoy the stillness of the water on the canals against the ancient buildings, while the youth played in the alleys. Music from church choirs could be heard in the distance.

I am here. I am truly here, in Venice.

10

IT'S ENOUGH TO MAKE A VENETIAN BLIND

In the United States, it was common to live somewhere for years and not even know your next-door neighbors. This, I believed, was because we would get into our car in the garage, open the garage door with the push of a button, and travel anonymously until we reached our destination, never giving ourselves the opportunity to communicate with others doing the same thing—with the notable exception of a few unpleasant hand gestures out the window.

In Venice, the city was like one big family. When a Venetian left home, he greeted the fishmonger selling the day's catch right outside his front door, waved at the baker, and stopped to ask the butcher about his family. Walking by a friend's café, bar, or store without stopping to chat was unthinkable. That made it almost impossible to get anywhere quickly. On a typical day, I would have four or five espressos on my way to the market, as every friend along the way wanted me to stop and have coffee with him. This requirement to take one hour to arrive at a destination which appeared to be ten minutes from your home was known as "The Venice Effect."

One evening, we received a call from Francesco at *Bar ai Miracoli* in Castello. "I'm leaving now and heading straight to your apartment for dinner." Francesco's bar was a ten-minute walk from our apartment. When he arrived over an hour later, I asked, "Francesco, what happened? You called over an hour ago."

"What did you expect? I'm Venetian. I know everybody along the way." Handing me a bottle, he said, "Here. Let's have some wine, and everything will be okay."

One morning while I was having coffee with Gino at his pastry shop, an older woman walked in and ordered coffee in Italian, but with a British accent. "You must meet my American friend," Gino told her, proudly introducing me as his dear friend, Giuseppe. We spoke for a few minutes and agreed to get together for dinner one evening.

Later that afternoon, across town, Viviana called to me as I passed by her electricity store. "You know the lady you met at Gino's this morning? Well, you forgot to get her phone number, and she asked me to give it to you." Taking the folded piece of paper from Viviana, I started to ask, "But how did you—"

"You're in Venice, Giuseppe. Here, everybody knows your business, sometimes even before you do! *Ciao!*"

Mailboxes Etc. – Part 3

I received a call from my brother in Florida who asked me if I could pick up some Mickey Mouse bowls for him at the Disney store in Padova, roughly an hour away from Venice. So, Debbie and I took the train to Padova and found the Disney store and the bowls, but the store wouldn't ship them back to the U.S. We brought them back to Venice, and I searched for packing materials I could use for shipping. Wandering around my neighborhood, I remembered that a few days earlier I had seen a storefront with packing materials strewn around the floor. I would stop there and ask.

The store looked vaguely familiar. Sure enough, it was the location which, for a brief period the previous year, had housed the ill-fated Mail Boxes Etc. store and my temporary address. While there were no signs of any mailboxes, and it was clearly a different store, the gentleman was happy to pack and ship my package.

When it came time to pay, he read the name on my credit card. "Frangipane? Barry Frangipane? I have been saving mail for you for almost a year!" It was Cesare. He went into the back and returned with a pile of mail, mostly junk, all addressed to me at box 101, all from early last year.

"How long will the package take to arrive in Florida?" I asked.

"*Non ti preoccupare.* The package will arrive in Florida within a week."

About a month later, when my brother called me to say that the box had never arrived, I returned to Cesare's new store. Happily, he was still in business, and his store was open. After a great deal of tracking and quite a few phone calls, he found the box. It was still sitting in a FedEx warehouse in Treviso, half an hour away. With a little coaxing from Cesare, the package was shipped, and my brother received it within a week.

Note: As I write this, a clothing store has replaced Cesare's latest shipping venture.

The Street Beggars

While walking the streets of Venice, one comes in frequent contact with beggars. They sit most often on the steps of the bridges with signs reading, "Please help. Two

Children. Need Food." The signs appear to all have been made by the same person, and the beggars seem to be of eastern European origin. There are roughly fifteen or twenty of them with similar clothing and facial features.

About two years earlier on a vacation in Venice, while walking near Francesco's *Bar ai Miracoli*, I saw a man begging for money. The man was similar to most of the beggars in Venice; he was not at all aggressive. He just sat there with a small dish in his outstretched hand. I stopped to learn more about him.

His name was Miloiko, and he came from ex-Yugoslavia. While his Italian was very poor, he managed to tell me that he was a sheet metal worker in nearby Yugoslavia. The NATO bombs had blown up his factory, and there was no longer any work in his town. He came to work in Italy, but without a work visa, neither he nor his wife Christina could get a job. Miloiko hoped to truly learn Italian and get the proper papers to work. On another day, I gave him a bag of groceries containing the essentials: Salami, cheese, bread, spaghetti, and spaghetti sauce. Then it occurred to me that he might not have a place to cook the spaghetti.

"We live on a boat. There are about sixteen of us living together trying to make it here. We have a camping stove for cooking, but no electricity and no running water. We have a small gas heater, but it gets pretty cold in the winter," he said. Later that day, I saw both Miloiko and Christina sitting on a bench eating lunch together before each returned to their respective bridges for their afternoon "work." They invited me to share lunch with them.

Further visits to Italy brought more conversations with Miloiko. He showed me pictures of his family, including his daughter who was studying in Yugoslavia to become a doctor. He gave me his home address in Yugoslavia, and I promised to write. His Italian was improving with each visit.

During another visit to Venice, Miloiko greeted me as I approached. "*Ciao, Giuseppe! E Deborah, come va?*" We would always ask each other about family. Christina was having problems with her ear and for the moment wasn't doing well.

"If she doesn't get better, we will return home," he said. "Sometimes it's better to be hungry and with your family than to be so far away with no one."

This year, one of my first stops was to Miloiko's bridge. He was missing. I returned every few days, but neither Miloiko nor Christina could be found. What had happened to them? Had the authorities kicked them out? Did Christina's ear get worse? How could I find out?

Remembering that so many of the beggars were "*barchini,*" boat people living together, I decided to ask Rosa, the lady who begged on the bridge over Rio Marin.

Rosa told me that Miloiko was doing well, but that he was staying with Christina who was in the hospital in Vicenza for an operation on her ear. Sure enough, a few weeks later, Miloiko and Christina both returned to their respective bridges. Miloiko inquired immediately about my wife and daughters by name. His Italian, like mine, had improved greatly. At that point, we could carry on a real conversation. He explained that a friend had let him and Christina stay in an apartment in Vicenza. They had light, heat, running water, and some food. It took them two and a half hours to get to Venice every day, and it was clear that he missed his home in Yugoslavia.

"We have been trying for years to get working papers with no luck. If things don't change in six months or so, we will go home. There are still very few jobs at home, but look at me here. I miss my family and beg on the streets. I am not a beggar. I want to go home. Someday my new country of Slovenia will become a full member of the European Union, and I will be able to work again. They keep saying that it will happen soon, but I don't know how long we can wait."

A week or so later, I returned to Rio Marin to see Rosa again. But a new lady had taken her place. "Rosa's husband was sick, and they returned to Yugoslavia," she said. "By the way, I am looking for an Italian husband. You don't know anyone I could marry, do you? Are you available?"

she asked. I explained that I was American, married, and didn't know any Italian bachelors to whom she could be introduced.

"If you find one, I'll be here," she assured me.

The next day in a different part of town, I saw another lady begging by a bridge near Campo San Barnaba. She was frequently stationed at that spot, and since I had some time, I went to the nearby grocery store, filled up a grocery bag with essentials and returned to the spot I had seen her, but she was gone. I looked in all directions but couldn't find her. Certain there would be another beggar along my route, I continued toward the Accademia. In the distance, I saw the lady beggar just sitting down on the steps of another bridge and putting out her sign, *"Please help. Two Children. Need food."* But there was also a burly, bearded beggar sitting directly opposite from her, who was obviously not happy that she had stationed herself on *his* bridge.

"Get off of my bridge!" he yelled at the elderly lady setting out her sign.

"I need a place too," she said.

"Then go find another bridge," the burly beggar demanded, as he yanked the elderly lady up by the arm and attempted to move her by force.

"Enough!" I yelled at the man. He seemed very surprised to see that I had witnessed the entire scene, and he backed off.

"It's okay now. Here are some groceries to get you by for today," I said to the lady.

She started to cry. "Thank you. Now if you could just tell *Il Capitano* of the bridge over there that I can stay here too, that would be wonderful!" she said. I shook my head in amazement and continued my walk to Castello to meet a friend.

Christina was in her usual spot on the steps of the bridge entering Campo Santa Maria Formosa. Cheery but cold, she asked about Deborah. I asked about her ear, which was recovering nicely, but she said that sitting outside on the cold concrete was not doing well for her health. "I miss my family, and I want to go home," she confided. At this point, we both had to move to the right a few feet, as there was an important photo shoot occurring on the bridge with a fashion model wearing the latest style from Milan leaning on the bridge as a makeup artist applied the final touches. I kissed Christina's forehead, which was wrinkled from the sun, wished her well, and walked away, being careful to avoid the electric cord powering the fan blowing the model's hair as the shutter clicked.

The Merchants of Venice

In Venice, as in many small towns in Italy, owning a store was as much about relationships as it was about making money. A few years back, on one of our month-long trips to Venice, my wife and I had purchased a hat from a tiny boutique, where we had conversed with the owner for a few minutes. Nothing too unusual there.

Roughly two weeks later, the day before our return to the United States, we realized we needed a box so that Debbie's hat wouldn't be ruined in the suitcase during the return trip. So, we returned to the shop.

The owner was so happy to see us again that she kissed each of us on the cheeks and invited us to the local café. Locking the front door of her store—with the "open" sign still displayed in the window—she walked us to the café four doors away. After buying us coffee, she sat down and said, "Tell me about your month in Venice. What were your favorite experiences? When will you return?"

We chatted for almost half an hour and exchanged addresses and phone numbers. We left feeling amazed at the warmth of the storeowner. "Come back again," she said. "I'm always open."

Living in Venice, we came to understand just how common it was to receive a warm, friendly welcome from people we had seen but once before. When a friend stopped into a store, the shopkeeper and the friend frequently headed to the local café, sometimes leaving the store both abandoned and unlocked. The relationships, it became clear, were far more important than any lost revenue.

Near our apartment was an *oreficeria*, gold jewelry shop, with an owner named Guido. Guido frequently sat outside his shop discussing politics with me, all the while watching the people walk by. One day, I walked by his shop in a rush to get to an appointment.

Guido called, "Giuseppe, *vien qua*. Come here." I followed him into his store, and he locked the door behind me. "Stay here," he said.

I thought, "Where on earth can I go? The door is locked, and the entire store is only five-by-ten feet." Guido returned from a small back room beaming with pride. In his hand was a Brownie-style Leica camera, circa 1940.

"Isn't she beautiful?" he asked. Admittedly, it was a nice camera. "I have had this camera for over fifty years," he said in a hushed tone. He took it apart and then re-assembled it, as if handling a priceless treasure.

Guido handed me a magazine from the 1940s. Not knowing why I had it in my hands, I gazed dumbly at the cover and then noticed his name in the lower right-hand corner of the cover page. "I took this photo with this camera," he explained. I congratulated him on his photo, whereupon he unlocked the door, and I headed to my appointment not caring that I was now thirty minutes late.

What was it that caused him on that day to close his store, pull out his camera, and share that piece of personal history with me? I might never know. What was clear, however, was that sharing this joy, sharing his shining triumph was far more important to him on that day than being open and making money.

In San Polo, a photograph in a store window caught my eye. It was a perfectly framed shot of a small bridge in Venice, with cherubs on the arches and grass growing in the cracks between the stones. The lighting was perfect, and no evidence of humanity distracted the eye from the bridge. I wanted that photo.

The store's front door, however, was locked, though the sign read, "Open 10-6 Monday through Saturday." It was eleven o'clock on a Wednesday morning, but there was no one in sight. I returned the following day at eleven thirty, but the door was once again locked.

Over the next few weeks, I would occasionally pass by the store, but it was always closed. Some of the photos in the window would be different, but there were no signs of humans anywhere. Finally, one morning at ten thirty, I noticed that the store was open. The owner/photographer hailed from Sweden and had married a Venetian. She explained this and her entire career in photography over coffee in the café down the block, while her store once again sat locked. From where I sat, I could see prospective customers tugging on the door, then checking their watches before walking away.

When we returned to the store, she said, "I will make you a copy of the print, and it will be ready for you this afternoon."

"But will you be um... open this afternoon?"

"Of course. From ten to six Monday through Saturday, I'm always open."

Festival of the Microscopic Snails

The phone rang. "*Ciao* Barry, *sono* Maxi." Maxi invited us to spend the day sailing in his twenty-five-foot boat, finishing the evening watching the celebration of *Il Redentore* and the fireworks over Venice, all from his boat in the lagoon.

La Festa del Redentore is a celebration held on the third Sunday every July to celebrate the miracle of *Il Redentore*, a church on the island of Giudecca. In the 1500s, there had been another episode of the plague in Venice, and almost one third of the population had succumbed to the disease. The church was built as thanks for delivering the city from the plague.

"Shall we bring anything?" I asked.

"Only drinking water. I have prepared dinner for *La Festa*. I'll be down to your apartment in thirty minutes, and we can walk to the marina," Maxi replied. Debbie and I hurriedly put together a bag with swimsuits, towels, water, and suntan lotion. It was a brief forty-minute walk from our apartment following Maxi and his shortcuts to Piazza San Marco, then down *Riva degli Schiavoni*, through *I Giardini*, past the soccer stadium and to the marina.

Maxi was an excellent sailor. He has written acclaimed articles on the Venetian Lagoon and spent years working for the organization that manages boat traffic around Venice. But today, Maxi was teaching Debbie and me how to sail. We sailed past Sant' Erasmo, and Maxi explained that many of the vegetables sold in Venice came from that island.

"Can we stop so I can swim?" I asked.

"No, not now. You must wait a few hours. Right now, the tide is leaving Venice and flushing out the canals. You don't want to swim in that water. In a few hours, the tide will be coming in from the Adriatic, and the water will be clearer."

As we headed through the channel toward the open water of the Adriatic, Maxi pointed out the man-made shoals which appeared to cut the width of the channel in half. "MOSE," Maxi said. "That's the grand Venetian plan to install underground barricades which can be raised when *Acqua Alta* would otherwise be imminent. The idea is that it will stop the flow of the tide and the force of the wind, which pushes the water into the lagoon and onto land. By reducing the width of the channel, they will need less of the expensive barricades."

Debbie interrupted, "Maxi, help! I'm sailing right into that big oil tanker!"

Maxi reassured her, "Deborah, *non ti preoccupare.* Just stay to the left and avoid hitting the shoal."

We sailed down the length of Lido Beach looking at the grand hotels, which in the 1940s were the required destination of celebrities making the popular world tour. Lido was also home to the annual Venice Film Festival.

As we re-entered the Venetian lagoon, the sun was setting over the islands and creating dark silhouettes of the countless bell towers. The cheese and bread we had for lunch were long gone, and Debbie and I were getting hungry. The lagoon was quickly filling up with everything from rowboats to sailboats to huge yachts, as mariners jockeyed for the best positions for viewing the upcoming fireworks.

Maxi put down the sails and dropped anchor. "Time to eat. I've prepared a Venetian specialty, *bovoeti.*" He gave us each a bowl and a toothpick. Then, from a large pot, he filled our bowls with snails. Not the "escargot" kind of snails to which we were accustomed, but snails so small that only a toothpick could be used to extract the microscopic piece of meat hidden inside. After pulling out five or ten of these tiny delicacies, I quietly mentioned to Debbie that we were most certainly burning more calories extracting these morsels than we could possibly be getting by eating them. As the fireworks lit up the sky, I contemplated jumping overboard to catch a fish for dinner.

Then, Maxi said, "And now, *Sarde in Saor*." He brought us plates of the traditional Venetian dish about which we had heard so much, but had never experienced. On our plates were sardines cooked in onions and sauteed in a vinegar sweet and sour sauce; Maxi had prepared them masterfully.

We savored our *Sarde in Saor* and enjoyed the fireworks, accompanied by music coming from live bands in Piazza San Marco. Our city, like an onion, had many layers. It had just displayed yet another one, thanks to Maxi.

Venice Happens

Stephanie and her boyfriend came to visit at our new apartment. Stephanie was excited to show him her parents' adopted hometown of Venice, but he had something even more important on his mind.

At the first possible moment, the boyfriend pulled us aside and asked for our daughter's hand in marriage. He was smart, handsome, and a fireman paramedic. What more could someone ask in a son-in-law? Without hesitation, we gave our approval. Then, he wanted to know how best to propose. He thought about proposing on a gondola, but that seemed almost commonplace. He wanted something special. That day was spent scoping out the entire town, searching for the perfect location, the perfect bridge, the perfect café, where he would pop the question to our daughter. Finally, he asked Debbie for help.

Debbie placed one phone call, and the plan was set. We were all to show up at the Venice Fire Station just across the bridge from Ca' Foscari at eleven thirty that evening. The *Vigile dei Fuoco*, or firemen, were good friends of ours, and they had met Stephanie on a previous visit. While disappointed that Stephanie was about to be engaged, they took solace in knowing that at least it would be to a fireman, even if not one of them.

We showed up promptly at the front door of the fire station. After giving the couple a tour of the fire station, one of the firemen put them in the captain's fireboat and sped off. Ten minutes later, under the Bridge of Sighs, Stephanie accepted the marriage proposal.

The next day at the local pizzeria, Tre Archi, the four of us sat outside reliving the previous day's events.

"I got engaged last night," Stephanie proclaimed to the waiter, "and to commemorate the day, I would like to purchase this Moretti Beer glass as a souvenir. Could I do that, please?"

"So, you are getting married. This is a cause for celebration." The waiter returned with two boxes of Moretti Beer glasses, twelve Coca-Cola glasses, and fifteen ice cream bowls. "This is a wedding present from us to you. Do you need a bag?"

When we left the pizzeria, Stephanie and I walked over to see my jeweler friend Guido, where I had left a ring to be sized about a week earlier.

"*Ciao*, Guido. How is my ring coming along?"

"I just finished it," he said, holding up the ring. "Look how I filled the inside with silver. Try it on." The ring fit perfectly.

"How much do I owe you?"

He stared at the ceiling for a moment, then offered, "Two euro?"

I checked my pockets, but all I had was a 50 euro note. I handed it over. "What's this?" he exclaimed. "Fifty euro? This is too big. I can't even use this to buy coffee." Handing me my ring, he added, "Giuseppe, here is your fifty euro, plus two euro in change. Now go buy your daughter a cup of coffee!"

Stephanie looked confused as we left the store. "What just happened, Dad?"

"It's Venice. Venice just happened."

11

LEAVING HOME

Gastone's Birthday

October was rapidly approaching, as was our return to the U.S. Gastone and I didn't speak of it much; our separation was something neither of us were looking forward to. "Come to Florida," I urged him.

"No, the doctors say that being at an altitude of over three thousand feet would be too hard on my heart, so I can't fly anymore." I looked into the possibility of his taking a cruise ship, but it just wasn't practical. So we continued our daily walks, pretending that they would last forever.

Gastone's eightieth birthday would be in September, and I wanted it to be special. He loved music and loved to hear it at La Fenice, Venice's opera house. But since his wife's death years ago, he had never left Cannaregio, except to take the boat every Sunday to Lido to visit her in the cemetery.

I did some checking with a friend who owned a water taxi. A taxi could pick us up at Gastone's apartment door on Rio Cannaregio and drop us off at the side door of La Fenice. The next day while walking with Gastone, I casually pointed to the poster in the window of the local *panificio.* "Concert at La Fenice Opera House Saturday September 12, 6:00 PM—All the old favorites," it read.

Gastone thought for a moment, and said sadly, "It sure looks wonderful, but I haven't been off the island in years."

I secretly called Greta, his German friend. She would come to Venice for the weekend of his birthday and go with us to La Fenice. With the tickets purchased, I arranged for the taxi, and waited for September twelfth to arrive.

The morning of Gastone's birthday, Greta told him that the three of us would be going to La Fenice. He was just starting to say, "But I haven't been off—" when Greta interrupted, "I don't want to hear it. Be ready at five thirty tonight."

I arrived at Gastone's apartment promptly. He answered the door in his best suit, standing up straighter than I had ever seen him stand, with a smile from ear to ear. As Greta appeared behind him, I said, "Happy birthday, Gastone! Let's go listen to some music!"

As the water taxi cruised slowly through the canals to La Fenice, I watched Gastone looking out the window at the town he knew so well, absorbing it all, reliving the memories. He insisted on getting his picture taken with Greta, then with me, then all together, outside La Fenice.

After he handed the usher our tickets, the three of us walked arm in arm into the theatre. Gastone's eyes were like that of a child on his first Christmas. It was the first time he had ever seen the new La Fenice, The Phoenix, rebuilt in 2003 after a fire had destroyed it in 1996. "It's just like the original. It's incredible."

During intermission, Greta got up to walk around, but Gastone stayed seated, looking around and taking it all in. "Those were some of my wife's favorite songs," he said, tears filling his eyes.

The rain was pouring when the performance was over, and the tide had risen so high that the water was level with the dock and soaked our shoes. I was a bit concerned with what being out in the rain, soaked from head to toe, might do to Gastone.

When the taxi arrived, we had another problem. The boat was now so high that we would have to climb into it. That would be a feat barely feasible for Greta and me, but impossible for Gastone. With me under one arm and the taxi driver under the other, Gastone was hoisted onto the boat, and we headed home soaking wet, but completely satisfied with our evening. As we said goodbye that night, Gastone hugged me so hard I thought he would never let go. We both knew that, as sure as the tide was now receding, our time together was coming to an end.

Saying Goodbyes

As the days got shorter, Debbie and I became preoccupied with thoughts we couldn't bring ourselves to discuss, thoughts of our impending departure from Venice and the return to the place we had previously thought of as home.

We had acquired so many things we didn't want to leave behind. Sure, there was the food processor, hand mixer, computer printer, and all the other electronics that would be impractical to transport to Florida; they wouldn't work on our U.S. current anyway. But the hardest things to leave behind were the people with whom we had developed friendships over the past year, and the slow, sensible, calming way of life.

We would miss the daily trips to the *fruttivendolo*, the fresh pasta, the artistry of the butcher, and the delicatessen where Freckles received a daily treat of Mortadella. I had grown attached to the name "Giuseppe" and was almost sad to return to being just Barry. We would miss Gino and his wonderful pastries at Il Bucintoro and Carlo's fresh flavorful gelato at Gelateria Alaska. I would miss my time with Gastone, the boys, and my evening walks along the quiet canals, while Debbie would miss her walks in the park with Freckles, talking to the locals, and sharing recipes and stories over *caffe corretto con grappa*. These were the things we most wanted to bring back, but would be forced to leave behind.

Over time, we shed our apartment of appliances no longer needed, giving the portable ones to Irene and Davide while donating others to the landlord. Each item removed from our apartment made our departure more imminent and more apparent.

A few weeks before we left, one last set of friends from the States came to visit. Heidi and Kristin, sisters from Florida, came to Venice hoping for one of Debbie's tours of the Veneto. After a few days of having Debbie take them around the islands, Kristin said, "Have you ever thought of doing this for a living?" But alas, our time in Venice was growing short, and we had promised friends and business partners that we would return after a year.

For Heidi and Kristin's last day in Venice, we decided to invite five or six of our Venetian friends for dinner, giving the sisters a chance to meet the locals, as well as giving us a chance to say goodbye to some of our friends over a meal.

Debbie would cook, and dinner would be served early, at eight o'clock, as Heidi and Kristin's water taxi would arrive at five in the morning to take them to the airport.

The three girls left the apartment at noon and headed for Murano. Boarding the vaporetto, Debbie looked back to find Heidi and Kristin at the back of a throng of tourists heading to the island of blown glass. Debbie motioned for them to move up to the front. "What about the line?" Heidi asked.

Debbie smiled knowingly. "This is Italy. There are no lines."

With sightseeing taking longer than planned, Debbie's meal wasn't ready until nine o'clock, which was perfect timing considering that all of the Italians arrived at nine, right on time, one hour after dinner was scheduled.

Maxi had brought his freshly steamed baby octopus from his apartment upstairs to share with the other guests. While Debbie and I were enjoying this Venetian delicacy, we watched the faces of the sisters as they attempted to eat even the smallest pieces of the food to which we had become accustomed over the past year. We ate, drank, and laughed until after one in the morning, before Gastone brought out his special grappa to close the evening. Four hours later, after loading the two sisters and their luggage into the water taxi, we couldn't help but notice the greenish tint of Kristin's face as the boat pulled away with her head over the side. "It must have been the octopus." We chuckled and headed back inside to pack.

Later that week, we stopped at "Bar da Tony" near the Rialto fish market to say goodbye to Tiziana, who along with her twin sister and father, Tony, owned the café and served *Illy* coffee, the best in Italy. To our surprise, Tiziana and her father were gone. In their place were Chinese immigrants, and the *Illy* coffee had been replaced with the more common *Lavazza*. The new owners had no idea where Tiziana and Tony had gone, and Tiziana's cell phone was no longer in service.

Where were the Venetians going? And why were some cafés being bought out by Chinese? A close Venetian friend explained,. "Life in Venice is getting tough for the Venetians," he said. "At the same time, it seems that the Chinese, now having money and wanting to pursue a better life for themselves and their families, are moving to the European Union. But moving to Italy isn't as simple as having money." Didn't we know that!

He continued, "But if a foreigner were to purchase a business, then the residency papers would be forthcoming. Cafés are an easy business to purchase, as they require little training to run, and little knowledge of the language. And our children do not want to work the fourteen-hour days, six days a week that a café requires, so some Venetians are selling the businesses and retiring."

He chuckled, "While life here may not be tough enough to make a Venetian blind, we do seem to be squinting more and more." Venice, it seemed, was continuing the tradition of giving people a chance at a better life.

We stopped by Rosetta and Renzo's bar to say goodbye. They had been friends of ours since our early trips to Venice, and we had coffee and pastries at their café every day before school. Rosetta poured us each a glass of wine, while Renzo passed out the pastries. We discussed the good times we had over the past year. When we got ready to leave, they hugged us both and, with tears in their eyes, waved goodbye.

The departure date now upon us, we had the last few dinners with friends and said goodbye to the family in Sarmede and Treviso. Gastone, who had had more than his share of goodbyes in his lifetime, didn't show up when Maxi and Mariella wished us farewell.

"He just doesn't like to say good-bye," Maxi explained. We were still receiving text messages from friends as we boarded our plane at Marco Polo airport with our twelve pieces of checked baggage and Freckles stowed safely below. As the plane took off, the pilot dipped the wing on our side, giving us one last look at Venice, our home, before turning away and heading over the Alps, back to the United States.

Our one-year experiment had been a success. Two average people with a house, pets, families, and jobs had up and left their home, moved to a foreign country, and had become part of the local family of Venice. We had made Venice our home. It was so simple; I wondered what had kept us from doing it for so long, and what kept others from ever trying it.

What we brought back with us was just as important as what we had left behind. We are forever changed, inspired by Venice and by its way of life, its serenity, and its sense of community. Troubles will visit us in life, as the *Acqua Alta* visits Venice, but as all Venetians know, the tides have a natural ebb and flow, and life soon returns to normal. As we learned each time we walked out of our Venetian apartment, it's not the destination that's important, it's the people we meet along the way that make all the difference. And no road, no *calle*, no canal seems too long, no tide too high, when friends line the way.

EPILOGUE

Two years after our return from Venice, Debbie and I started our travel business, Savory Adventures. For almost three years, Savory Adventures took small groups of travelers to Italy for week-long vacations. We stayed at villas normally rented by Hollywood stars. Debbie cooked for the guests—no more than six couples per trip—while I played the role of travel host.

This experience gave Debbie the confidence to pursue yet another dream, that of becoming a professional chef. After training at the prestigious Culinary Institute of America, she has taken on the stage name of *Dolce Debbie* and now conducts cooking shows, talks about food live on the radio, and is frequently featured on national television.

As for me, I have begun to write more. I am thoroughly enjoying the process of documenting our experiences in Italy and elsewhere, our story of pursuing and living a dream.

But somehow, with everything we have going on, friends and neighbors have taken on a more important role in our lives, and we relax more. I can just imagine Alfieri commenting on the fast pace of life outside Venice. "If they want to race around like crazy, let them. How about we talk about it over a glass of wine?"

This past winter, while Debbie was attending culinary school, I planned a quick trip to Venice, *La Serenissima*, both to catch up with old friends and to fact check certain portions of this book. All of the hotels in Venice were booked for Carnevale, so I checked with our friend Giorgio to see if I could stay with him. Giorgio, born and raised in Venice, now spends most of the year in Florida handcrafting exquisite masks at Disney's EPCOT center. He returns home each year to help his mother make and sell masks during Carnevale, and then again in September as an award-winning photographer for the Venice Film Festival.

"Giorgio, I need your help. I'm finishing my book and would like to return to Venice for the week of Carnevale, but every hotel is booked. I need a place to stay. Since you'll be in town, can I stay with you?"

"You can stay with my aunt," Giorgio offered. "She lives on the mainland in Mestre-Gazzera and has a spare bedroom."

We arranged everything with his aunt Lucilla, who picked me up at Venice's Marco Polo airport. In her car, she looked at me in wonder and asked why I was putting on my seat belt. "We Italians hate seat belts. But there is this law. So whenever we see a police officer, we pull it down like this, and Zing! We let go as soon as we have passed the police. You Americans are all so straight and proper, seat belts on, always stopping at lights, how strange!" Admittedly, it was a bit hard to hear Lucilla due to a constant "ding ding" coming from the car. "My last car was much better than this new one," she said. "This one beeps all the time just because I don't wear the seatbelt. Isn't it annoying?"

Arriving at the apartment, I was happy the dinging had ended. Lucilla showed me how the hot water worked in the bathroom. "You would think that the hot water would be on the left and the cold water on the right, as it is marked. But actually, it is reversed. Oh, and the hot water barely comes out; I think that there is, how do you say, calcium in the pipes. But fixing it would require a technician."

"I always keep this space heater on in the bathroom. It keeps the temperature above sixty degrees. There is also a hair dryer. But whatever you do, don't use the hair dryer while the space heater is on, or the main circuit breaker will blow. But when it does, you can reset it in the hallway."

The long overnight flight and the sub-freezing January temperature gave me reason enough to take a nice hot shower, but I couldn't remove the drain plug from the tub. I decided to wash in the sink. The hot water stayed on just long enough to wet my hair and add shampoo, but then became ice cold again when time to rinse. Freezing, I rinsed off and dried as quickly as I could. I reached for the hair dryer, and then remembered Lucilla's words. I dried my hair as best I could with the towel and left the bathroom.

"You didn't try to use the tub, did you?" Lucilla asked. "The drain only worked for the first two days after I moved in, and it hasn't worked since. And the hot water, isn't it amazing how quickly it gets cold? I called a technician a long time ago. Someday he will fix it."

I left Lucilla's apartment for the trip to Venice. The trip involved a one-mile walk to the bus stop, a thirty-minute bus ride to the Venice Mestre train station, then a ten-minute train ride to Venice. It was a cold, windy walk to the bus stop. Lucilla had given me a bus ticket. "This ticket is either good for ten rides, or it is all used up, I am not sure."

On board the bus, I held the ticket up to the new electronic machine, and the red light came on, indicating that the ticket was no good. The bus driver then explained that due to a new regulation, riders could no longer purchase a bus ticket from him. A pair of elderly ladies chastised me for getting on the bus and assured me that I would be getting a hefty fine of roughly fifty dollars when the bus police boarded the bus. "As they most certainly will. They check tickets all the time," one of them stated sternly.

The bus driver stopped at the next stop and said, "Get out here, and you can buy a ticket at the *tabaccheria*. The next bus will be here in thirty minutes." The *tabaccheria* is typically a very small store selling tobacco, newspapers, and tickets for the bus or train. I got out, and as the bus drove away, noticed that the store was closed for lunch. I walked the remaining mile to the train station.

The sign at the station indicated that the next train to Venice was leaving in less than one minute. I asked the conductor leaning out of the train door how much it would cost to purchase a ticket onboard for the ten-minute ride to Venice. "Fifty-one euro," came the reply.

"Fifty-one euro? But it's a ten-minute ride" I said.

"It's one euro for the ticket, and fifty euro for the fine if you board the train without a ticket! *Ciao!*" The conductor chuckled as the train pulled away from the station.

Arriving in Venice on the next train, I purchased a ticket good for one week of unlimited rides on the boats of Venice as well as the buses of Mestre. That evening, after returning to the Mestre train station, I boarded the bus back to Lucilla's apartment. The machine once again said that my ticket was no good.

"The machines always say that," the ticket seller said the next day in Venice. "Your ticket is good for a week. *Non ti preoccupare.* The new machines just don't work as well as the old ones did."

In Lucilla's apartment, I found her showing the apartment to a realtor. Evidently, it was going to be easier for her to move than to get the plumber to finish the job.

My return trip to the city of water, the city that has now survived for over sixteen hundred years, went by quickly. Venice, as it always has, continues to evolve. Some things evolve gradually, others at an ever-increasing pace.

The ticket-punching machines still don't work at the Venice train station, but no one seems to check the tickets on local trains anyway, so the system still works.

The fake purses are still sold on the streets, but the Moroccans have mostly been displaced by other nationalities selling them. On the other hand, all traces of the warnings that tourists would be prosecuted for purchasing these illegal purses have been removed.

Customers are no longer fined if they haven't received a valid receipt from the storekeeper. But the merchants are still fined if they don't provide the receipt.

It was a rainy week for Carnevale, but sales at my friend Giorgio's mask booth at the outdoor market in Campo Santo Stefano were brisk. Crowds filled Piazza San Marco to watch the annual flight of the angel, *il volo dell'angelo*, where someone, usually a celebrity, flies on a guide wire from the bell tower to the Doge's palace dressed in white, to celebrate the start of Carnevale. Venice's largest square was filled with masked revelers watching concerts on a stage erected in the center. Side *calli* were filled with vendors selling chestnuts, chocolates and, yes, even crepes.

I stopped at Il Bucintoro for pastries and to visit our friends Gino and Anna Maria. They looked even more tired than usual. It was the week of Carnevale, and the town had many tourists for the major event of the year for Venice. Gino stopped briefly, poured two glasses of Prosecco, and toasted to our friendship. Before returning to the crowd of tourists waiting to taste his pastries, he made sure I had rum cakes to bring home to Debbie and cookies for Freckles.

On to visit our dear friends Simone and Gloria who run the *alimentari*, or delicatessen, in Campo dei Miracoli. I arrived only to find a gift store of Murano glass in its place. Happily, Simone and Gloria were running the new store. "This is so much easier," Gloria said. "We work less hours and have less stress." They looked ten years younger.

"My family goes back many generations making Murano Glass," Gloria continued. And I used to make jewelry like this years ago."

A few doors down, Francesco's *Bar ai Miracoli* was bustling, as Francesco stood outside and greeted the pretty women walking by, occasionally putting down his cigarette to help out in the bar.

Visiting our old section of Cannaregio, I was pleased to see that the *Trattoria Dalla Marisa* was alive and busy with locals. I went in for lunch. Marisa was serving pasta with meat sauce followed by zucchini with Pecorino Romano cheese, a choice of thin steak or chicken breast, then *Sarde in Saor*, greens, and of course, wine and water. The waitress turned up the music loud when an old song came on and danced in the crowded aisle with the customers.

Outside a nearby restaurant, propped up on a lone chair, was a small piece of wood with nothing but the two words "*Poenta Pesse*" written in chalk. Chuckling, I translated from Venetian into Italian, "*Polenta e Pesce*," or "Seafood and Grits."

Guido retired, and his *Orificeria*—jewelry store—has been transformed into a shoe store offering the latest styles for young Venetians.

Gastone, my dear old Egyptian friend, still visits the grave of his Jewish wife once a week, but otherwise stays inside, blaming it on the weather.

Maxi, his son, has retired from the Venice maritime authority and is active in the Venice Yacht Club. He sails his boat across the Adriatic, always returning home to Venice in time to help out with local boating events, like the Regatta Storica.

With reggae music blasting, Carlo once again tried to convince me to try his *zenzero* gelato, but I settled for the pear gelato instead. "Where is Deborah?" he asked almost immediately.

The construction work outside our first apartment has finally concluded. In fact, I discovered this while going to my friend Viviana's electricity store to check on her and her husband. Her husband was the electrician who would someday return to finish the wiring in our second apartment. But the store had been replaced by a sales center for a new apartment building a few doors down from our first apartment. I visited the complex—after suffering through the noise of the construction, it seemed only fitting—to find beautiful new apartments ready to fulfill other people's dreams of living in the city of water.

Carmelo, who ran the *Torrefazione* since the 1950s, had died, and the coffee shop had been passed down to the next generation, in the same way that Carmelo had inherited it from his father before him. The locals continued to drink their espresso while leaning or sitting on fifty-pound bags of coffee beans.

After almost a thousand years, the fraternity of male gondoliers has its first female *gondolier*. A twenty-three-year-old mother of two has followed her father's footsteps and passed the rigorous examination to become the first woman in Venice's history to join the almost five hundred men proud to call themselves *gondoliers*.

Davide and Irene have had their child, Geremia, and left Venice. Their apartment was a ground-floor apartment, and they felt it wasn't healthy for the baby. They now live in Rovigo, forty-five minutes away, but visit Venice frequently.

And the elderly are still holding on. They still go to the markets every morning, even in bad weather when the umbrellas are turned inside out by the wind. MOSE, the project to protect the city from the worst of the floods, has started construction. Whether or not it will ever be finished is still up for debate. Meanwhile, *Acqua Alta* continues.

And yet some things don't change. The traghetti still ferry locals back and forth across the Grand Canal, and the tourists still overpay for gondola rides. The old man at the Rialto fish market still sings every day. The young man selling his vegetables there still shouts out their virtues to entice passersby. Merchant boats still ignore the speed limit, occasionally sending a gondolier and his passengers into the canal.

After having been missing for years, I showed up at ten thirty in the morning, as I used to do, at the *Torrefazione* for coffee with the boys.

"Sorry, I'm late," I said, noticing that they were already standing at the counter having their coffee.

"It's okay, Frangipane, but it's your turn to pay," Franco said, barely turning around.

"*Vabbe,*" I said, proud to have a chance to use my Venetian dialect. I pulled out my old punch card with five punches left. The aroma of the coffee beans being roasted in the rear of the store filled the air as I leaned on the counter sipping my macchiato. The boys and I discussed today's visit to the bakery, the butcher, and the vegetable market.

BIBLIOGRAPHY

Boulton, Susie, and Christopher Catling. 2001. *Venice and the Veneto*. Dorling Kindersley Publishing.

Casanova, Giacomo. 1838. *Histoire de Ma Vie*. Laforgue.

Fuga, Guido, and Lele Vianello. 2005. *The Secret Venice of Corto Maltese*. Lizard Edizioni.

Oliphant, Margaret. 2008. *The Makers of Venice*. Homewood.

Scibilia, Michela. 2004. *Venice Botteghe*. Vianello Libri.

Vitoux, Frederic. 1991. *Venice, the Art of Living*. Stewart, Tabori & Chang.

USEFUL ADDRESSES

Gelateria Alaska
Calle Larga Dei Bari
Santa Croce 1159

Pasticceria Dal Nono Colussi
Calle Lunga San Barnaba
Dorsoduro 2867a

Torrefazione
Marchi Caffe Costarica
Rio Tera San Leonardo
Cannaregio 1337

Trattoria Dalla Marisa
Cannaregio, 652b

Pasticceria Il Bucintoro
Calle del Scaleter
San Polo 2229

Bar ai Miracoli
Campo Santa Maria Nova
Cannaregio 6066

Trattoria Casa Mia
Calle dell'Oca
Cannaregio 4430

Imagina Café
Campo Santa Margherita
Dorsoduro 3126

Museum of Natural History
Fondago dei Turchi
Santa Croce, 1730

ABOUT THE AUTHORS

Barry Frangipane, a native of Florida, hosts luxury vacations to Italy. While he has read many Pulitzer Prize winning novels, this is his first attempt at writing one. He is very proud that his new book exemplifies the writing style of Ernest Hemingway, in that both of their books contain multiple words combined to form sentences, and occasionally even paragraphs. He knows English, Italian, French, and the names of many other languages.

Ben Robbins, also a Florida native, has slightly better punctuation skills than his co-author. A writer most of his career, he is now a published author. He knows this because his name is on the cover of this book. When not writing books, he enjoys traveling with his family, exploring the outdoors and working two jobs to pay the bills. He takes great pride in being extraordinarily humble, but of course would not want you to know that.